"In a time of rapid and profound change, one of the greatest risks leaders face is listening only to voices that confirm their own views. . . . Saj-nicole Joni has given us a remarkable book to help overcome this systemic blindness. The Third Opinion *is rich in ideas, tools, examples, and inspiration."*

—Peter Schwartz, author of *The Art of the Long View*

"Reveals for the first time an entirely new dimension to executive leadership. [This book is] fun, informative, and very thought-provoking."

—Carter McClelland, president, Banc of America Securities

"Highly readable, practical, and penetrating."

—Nathaniel Mass, former senior vice president, Gencorp; partner, McKinsey and Company

"This is a very important breakthrough book on a topic that many have talked about but no one has [explained] in as clear, accurate, and helpful a manner as has Dr. Joni. With her guidance, we have a very real sense of what an advisory network looks like, how we can build one, and what it can enable in our professional—and personal—lives."

—Stuart Sadick, managing partner, Heidrick and Struggles

"A must-read book for executives who seek to improve the effectiveness of their leadership and management."

—Daniel Steiner, president, New England Conservatory of Music

"Provides a workable and structured way to deal with the basic dilemma that every manager and executive faces every day—getting an accurate picture of what is actually happening inside and outside the organization."

—Patrick Ellingsworth, head of group taxation and corporate structure, Royal Dutch/Shell

"Required reading for the leaders of today and tomorrow who aspire to lead successful organizations."

—Ed Hotard, former president and COO, Praxair, Inc.

"Dr. Joni's leadership habits of mind, relationship, and focus are practices that will enhance success for twenty-first-century leaders."

—Nancy J. Hutson, Ph.D., senior vice president, Pfizer Global Research and Development; director, Groton/New London Laboratories

"[The Third Opinion] *presents a wonderful system [that will show you] how to enrich your leadership circle with people who can help you make the right decision."*

—John M. Connolly, vice president, IBM Corporation

"A real contribution to the management literature."

—Dan Ciampa, author of *Right from the Start*

THE THIRD OPINION

THE THIRD OPINION

How Successful Leaders Use Outside Insight to Create Superior Results

Saj-nicole A. Joni, Ph.D.

PORTFOLIO

PORTFOLIO
Published by the Penguin Group
Penguin Group (USA) Inc., 375 Hudson Street, New York, New York 10014, U.S.A.
Penguin Books Ltd, 80 Strand, London WC2R 0RL, England
Penguin Books Australia Ltd, 250 Camberwell Road,
Camberwell, Victoria 3124, Australia
Penguin Books Canada Ltd, 10 Alcorn Avenue, Toronto, Ontario, Canada M4V 3B2
Penguin Books India (P) Ltd, 11 Community Centre, Panchsheel Park,
New Delhi–110 017, India
Penguin Books (N.Z.) Ltd, Cnr Rosedale and Airborne Roads,
Albany, Auckland, New Zealand
Penguin Books (South Africa) (Pty) Ltd, 24 Sturdee Avenue,
Rosebank, Johannesburg 2196, South Africa

Penguin Books Ltd, Registered Offices: 80 Strand, London WC2R 0RL, England

First published in 2004 by Portfolio, a member of Penguin Group (USA) Inc.

1 3 5 7 9 10 8 6 4 2

LIBRARY OF CONGRESS CATALOGING-IN-PUBLICATION DATA
Joni, Saj-nicole A.
The third opinion : how successful leaders use outside insight to create superior results / Saj-nicole A. Joni.
p. cm.
Includes index.
ISBN 1-59184-009-0 (cloth)
1. Leadership. I. Title
HD57.7.J665 2004
658.4'092—dc22 2003061023

This book is printed on acid-free paper. ♾

Printed in the United States of America

To Dick and Daren,

whose untimely passings
remind us
to live to our full capacity,
with sails unfurled

ACKNOWLEDGMENTS

This book could not have been written without the contributions and encouragement of many people.

First and foremost, I would like to thank my many clients in companies across the globe, the extensive list of leaders who agreed to be interviewed for this book, and my colleagues at Microsoft, Index, and MIT. You have generously given your time, shared your experiences and knowledge, and granted me the opportunity to develop the insights contained herein.

Laureen Rowland believed in this work from its inception. Even before I had written the proposal, she felt this was a book that needed to be published. As my agent, mentor, and confidante, Laureen made this book possible, helping me find a path forward through some difficult terrain along the way. Thanks also to David Black for his leadership, guidance, and support.

I am deeply grateful to Joe Fuller for his generous and timely support of my work. Joe exemplifies the best there is in a thinking partner: insightful questions, ability to think in broad contexts, commitment to ideas, and a wonderful sense of humor. Along with a Monitor Group grant to support the research for this book, Joe made himself, his leadership team, and the many resources of the Monitor Group available to me during the formative stages of this work. To him, and to the people of Monitor, my deepest thanks.

This book would not have been possible without Nick Morgan. His prodigious talent as a writer, his belief in the importance of these insights, his ability to serve as an intellectual foil, his clarity, and his commitment were all called upon in writing this book. I am honored and grateful for our collaboration and partnership.

Special thanks go to the members of my research and writing team: Nathan Furr, Amanda Hickman, Tammy Hobbs-Miracky, Sandy Hook, Bill Patrick, Nikki Smith, and Melissa Zervoudis. They were instrumental in getting this done, working long hours, with great energy, enthusiasm, and wit.

There are many people who have profoundly shaped my thinking over the years. While it is not possible to name them all, I would like to acknowledge and thank Tony Athos, Gordon Bell, Donald Berman, Jim Champy, Patricia Chew, Dave Cunningham, Bill Gates, Evelynn Hammonds, Inge Hoffman, M. Kanai Sensei, Alan Kay, Dawna Markova, Nicholas Negroponte, Jeff Raikes, Gian-Carlo Rota, Peter Senge, Patti Stonesifer, Erling Sunde, Polly van der Linde, Jan van der Wal, Stephen Warschawski, Marya Weinstock, Carl Wolf, and Patricia Zander.

Thanks also go to colleagues and friends who have listened, argued, and encouraged me in the development of this work: Don Arnoudse, Gaurdie Banister, Tom Barocci, Judy Brown, Dan Ciampa, Tom Ehrenfeld, Liam Fahey, Marc Gamson, Ed Hotard, Harry Hutson, Michael Jensen, Alan Kantrow, John Kennedy, Nat Mass, Karen Otazo, Stuart Saddick, Rich Schroth, Wanda Wallace, Fred Wiersema.

Adrian Zackheim, Stephanie Land, and Megan Casey at Portfolio have been a wonderful team to work with. The book is immeasurably better for their efforts and guidance.

Finally, for their love, encouragement, and patience as I devoted so much time and energy to this book, I would like to thank my parents, Daniel and Thelma, and family, Patricia, Carol Anne, Clifford, Darlene, Sheldon, Eric, Stephanie, Liz, Alicia, Tamara, Joe, Caitlin, and Alec.

CONTENTS

INTRODUCTION

This book is about leadership and the crucial role of the third opinion. It's about filling your leadership circles with the right expertise, wisdom, honesty, and diversity of view, creating an advisory network that can help you stretch beyond your individual reach. And it's about building the leadership circle that makes it possible for you to raise your bar of ambition and success—no matter how famous you are, or how insightful, or how often right.

This is what it takes to lead today: commitment, intelligence, compassion, curiosity, courage—and the wisdom of others.

Modern-day leaders have more to know and less time to learn than their predecessors. The pressure to act swiftly is relentless. It's likely that you are managing an increasing number of diverse areas that you need to understand and integrate if you are to excel at your job. Customer demands are greater than before, and there's a stronger sense of urgency to perform. Today's leaders must respond to quick-paced global marketplaces, ceaseless innovation, and a whole host of issues they cannot control.

Given these challenges, you simply must be operating at peak capacity—every minute.

What enables people to reach and sustain peak performance? Training and coaching are key developmental tools, but they're not enough. You can't realize your full potential alone. And you cannot sustain full potential alone. The best leaders know this. Throughout history, great leaders have surrounded themselves with advisers, mentors, intellectual sparring partners, and confidants. *Working with a circle of the best thinkers—as advisers, experts, and questioners—is essential to successful leadership.*

Yet your inner circle must offer you more than expertise. It must also create trust and an external perspective to help you see what others around you are missing. Most executives understand how important it is to be able to accurately judge the personal trustworthiness of employees, colleagues, and bosses. Leaders also learn with time to calibrate quickly their trust levels of the experts whose advice they regularly need on many subjects, from markets to technology to the law. But there's a third kind of trust that's less well understood, one that trips leaders up all too often and that can even derail their careers: *structural trust.*

Structural trust is about the ways that job roles affect business relationships and their trust levels. Are people in roles where their judgment is likely to be significantly influenced by their need to advance their own self-interest? In light of their roles, are they structurally able (vs. personally able or willing) to be fully forthcoming and loyal?

Using outside insight does not imply any weakness in your organization's talent pools. And it's not something that can be bought on a moment's notice. A robust leadership circle is one that draws upon the best of your internal and external relationships. Particularly when you are thinking through tough issues, you can't suddenly hire this kind of loyalty, discretion, and access to expertise. You can only build it, one step, one relationship, at a time.

▼

I didn't set out to become an adviser and thinking partner, working with business leaders around the globe to develop outside insight on the challenges they face. This aspect of my work didn't begin until after I had already had several successful careers: as a scientist, university professor, and senior business executive. I'm now the person leaders turn to after they've gotten second-opinion advice and feedback from key people within their organizations and extended teams. I'm the third opinion—the person they turn to with their most confidential questions, risks, and uncertainties. As a thinking partner, I help them develop alternatives and solutions. I provide outside perspective so that we can test their ideas, tear those ideas apart, looking for errors in information or missing pieces in logic, and put them back together again. The process allows these leaders to vet the tough calls while continuing to drive leaps in performance.

I've served in this role for more than ten years, and over that time, it has become evident to me that a few talented leaders naturally know how to assemble their advisory networks and incorporate them into their leadership team as powerful and well-utilized resources. But many promising leaders do not. In 2001, funded in part by a grant from the Monitor Group, I undertook a research project to understand the dynamics of leaders and their advisory networks, and to unlock the secrets of this powerful but, for many, elusive leadership resource.

For three years, I interviewed hundreds of executives and their advisers and thinking partners in order to understand these issues in depth. My research has led to two insights that form the heart of this book:

Insight 1: Leadership today requires three new habits—Habit of Mind, Habit of Relationship, and Habit of Focus. Used together, these Habits will enable you to build a powerful leadership circle and take advantage of the benefits of outside insight. These Habits are vitally important to the kind of leader you will be. They will distinguish your leadership and your career trajectory.

Insight 2: You can start developing the three Habits and your advisory network at any time during your career. It's important to develop and use the three Habits in concert. While everyone will use them differently, there are guidelines to help you focus on perfecting the various parts of each habit as your leadership progresses.

But how do you find the right people with whom to develop the third opinion? How can you be sure you've assembled the best advisory network for your needs? This book is the practical guide to building the most powerful leadership team possible at each stage of your career. In Chapter 1 we will explore the essence of outside insight for business leaders. Studying examples of leaders at all levels, we will, in Chapter 2, give an overview of the three Habits—of Mind, Relationship, and Focus—that you must develop to successfully form an inner circle capable of finding and using the third opinion as an integral part of decision making. Then, in Chapters 3, 4, and 5, we will take up the full discussion of each habit in turn.

The models for developing your inquiry team vary depending on your career level and responsibilities. It's likely that you already have some sort of advisory network, though it may not be well developed or optimally tuned to your current leadership challenges.

Regardless of who you are—Early Leader, Key Leader, or Senior Leader—this book can help. Indeed, small business owners and leaders in government, not-for-profits, and educational institutions will find the insights in this book useful as well.

In Chapters 6 through 9, we will show you how to create the unique network of resources that is required for your particular leadership challenges. We will discuss how to develop and use the most important aspects of each Habit at the different leadership stages of your career. Along the way we will outline a sequential set of practical steps, tools, and questions to guide you on your leadership journey.

▼

Even with the normal tensions of competition and turf within organizations, people have a great stake in the success of their leaders. They are counting on their leaders' abilities to focus on the long-term, non-urgent, yet important issues in the broadest contexts with the best and most challenging thinking. A key factor in how employees at all levels perceive senior leaders is how broadly senior leaders think, whom they think with, and how committed they are to learning and change.

And yet one of the surprises in my research is the level of isolation that leaders at all levels are experiencing. While some leaders find a way to build trusted leadership circles that integrate outside insight and have a few confidants, many are on the other end of the spectrum and only experience greater isolation with each move up the leadership ladder.

Your full leadership circle is personal, unique, and critical to your success. My goal is to give leaders at all levels an insightful and practical guide to developing the fully powered leadership circle that is right for you. Throughout this book, we will be working with real stories of real leaders—disguised for reasons of confidentiality—who have faced a range of issues and challenges.

You will meet Matthew, who faces an accounting issue that suddenly threatens to become page-one news. He needs to move quickly, but does he take the story public or keep it close? You will meet Alyce, whose career in Operations has jump-shifted to the vice-presidential level and who suddenly has to learn to think in very new ways and to deal with pressing issues of structural trust. You will meet Jim, who finds an accidental thinking partner when he is assigned to run an overseas division and loses that thinking partner when he is brought back to run the entire U.S. division. He finds that his traditional leadership circle is no longer adequate. How does he recruit the thinking partners he now needs? And you will meet Andy, who gets the chance to run a division, after having worked his way up in headquarters roles. How can he win the trust of the line people he's working with now and deal with issues that previously had been mostly theoretical for him?

Taken together, the stories in this book cover a broad spectrum of issues that confront leaders today. As we explore these stories, we will see how the Habits of Mind, Relationship, and Focus work in real situations. We will see how advisory relationships develop, move, and change over time. And we'll see the enormous impact, in both business and personal terms, of key thinking partner relationships and the power of outside insight.

CHAPTER 1

The Essence of Outside Insight

Matthew Whalen picked up *The Wall Street Journal,* scanned the front-page news, and broke out in a cold sweat. A high-flying manufacturing company had participated in a series of investments that fraudulently disguised debt. One of the financial deals mentioned was familiar to Matt. Too familiar.

Matt settled back in his chair, steepling his fingers, his eyes straying to the floor-to-ceiling windows of his corner office and the impressive view of New York City beyond. He loved his job and the perks that still went with it. But that day he had a feeling he was going to grow a few gray hairs.

Some months ago, long before the stunning collapse of the high flyer, Matt learned that his firm had participated with several other firms in one of these debt-concealing investments. As the transaction wended its way through the usual checks and balances of his company's accounting and assurance process, it had ended up on his desk. After a thorough review, Matt concluded that the transaction looked like a loan in funny clothing and made sure it was properly accounted for as debt. This of course made the transaction an unnecessarily costly way to achieve debt financing for the company, but Matt was confident it was the conservative and appropriate choice. As senior vice president of U.S. Finance for a global commodities company, Matt was used to making these calls.

But now the media was having a feeding frenzy for even the faintest taste of corporate financial irregularities. His firm had worked hard to maintain its reputation as a highly ethical company that did things the right way for the right reasons. But no one this size was perfect.

The last thing Matt wanted was for this thing to blow up in the press. Even though he knew the corporation was technically clean on the transaction, he also knew the power of perception. If the company got dragged into the media spotlight on this issue, it could suffer even though it had done nothing improper.

Matt was pretty sure that the folks at global headquarters had no idea their U.S. subsidiary was involved in this transaction. In fact, he wasn't sure who in his firm knew. The lead person on the team who did the deal had since joined another firm. The auditor hadn't flagged anything—probably because of the conservative way Matt handled it. It wasn't a secret, but if it became known, especially in the current climate, it wouldn't be good news. He didn't know if the press knew all the investors in the deal, or what they would do if they did know. He thought it was privileged information, but that wouldn't help if it got out anyway.

Thoughts raced through Matt's mind. Could he stop it? Mitigate it? Could he handle it by being there first, disclosing the truth before it was reported inaccurately? Wouldn't that look suspicious and create exactly what he was trying to prevent? If he ignored it, would it go away? Was that wise, prudent, or just plain stupid? As head of U.S. Finance, what was his role in handling this? How and when did global HQ need to know? How could he frame the issue and its context so that he wouldn't alarm people in his own firm who might not handle this in the best way? He wasn't afraid of making the hard calls—but should he handle this one or pass it up to someone else? Was this a real crisis or a time for "steady at the helm"?

Matt was sure of one thing. The issue was complex, the stakes high. He knew this situation warranted pushing his own thinking hard and fast to see if he had missed any angle. He turned instinctively around in his chair as if to talk with someone—and then remembered that he was top dog now. He did his best thinking out loud, bouncing ideas off someone else, but whom could he talk to?

He wanted to thrash it out with someone who knew him, knew the firm, and had lots of experience under fire. Was there somebody on his staff? But he wanted someone who had no self-interest in the outcome. That ruled out his boss, too. And colleagues at equivalent positions around the globe. A call to one of them would probably flush the issue out in the open, because of the responsibilities that went with their roles. He was annoyed, a little overwhelmed, and under the gun. He reached for the phone.

The Complexity of Modern Leadership Demands New Thinking

Matt's problem is hardly unique. The twenty-first century has dawned, and something profound has happened: the requirements for leadership have fundamentally changed. Day after day, leaders around the globe face issues of complexity, uncertainty, and sensitivity, requiring precise thinking and judgment at warp speed. It has been a series of incremental changes, rather than a management Big Bang, but the incremental changes have accumulated over the years and finally pushed us into a new era.

In short, from the earliest stages of one's career, the leadership bar has been raised:

Speed is a given—and it has changed more than just time.

Many business processes are not just faster, they are fundamentally altered by operating in real time or near–real time. Technology has allowed for near-instant feedback. What still yields competitive advantage when your pricing, product mix, and game plan are known to competitors and customers alike?

Expertise is fleeting.

Most careers now require that people be able to learn, function, and lead in areas well beyond their educational background and experience. The half-life of expert knowledge is shorter than ever before.

Learning to deal with trust issues in an environment of change is trickier than ever.

Simultaneous cooperation and competition make for tricky navigation in the waters of trust. This is true at all levels: individual, intraorganizational, and external partnerships.

Cross-industry change and competition is the name of the game.

The rapid lowering of barriers to entry in many industries, the emergence of information and service in most product categories, and the increase of global interdependencies all lead to new threats, new mergers, and new forms of competition and opportunity.

Maintaining a profit margin is increasingly a matter of complexity.

Business is no longer a matter of simply pounding out the same widget or dealing with the same "billable buddies." The competitive landscape is continually being redrawn, with temporary advantage shifting to a new competitor each time someone discovers how to exploit a new level of complexity in the offering. Maintaining your profit margins is increasingly a matter of being able to outplay your competitors in the complexity game.

Globalization is the norm in every business.

It's a given that in order to survive and indeed thrive, you will have to do business in countries outside your own, with customs you're unfamiliar with, and across multiple languages. Globalization means much greater interdependence of goods, economies, and risks.

Information and network complexity have increased.

There's an overwhelming information deluge hitting everyone in the organization, creating increasingly complex relationships, boundaries, constituencies, geopolitical realities, and technological innovation. In today's networked environment, being able to see several moves ahead is critical.

Authority has given way to influence.

The shared information and distributed decision making that began in software and financial services are now virtually everywhere, because every business today is, to some extent, information-based. Accordingly, leaders must get their organizations and their partners' organizations to work together by exerting influence rather than solely by exercising authority in some prescribed sphere.

New technologies continuously disrupt marketplaces.
Moore's Law still prevails, and Moore-like laws extend well beyond the size of microchips to govern the pace of scientific discovery and technical innovation in many arenas. Relentless scientific innovation will continue to foster disruptive change that will transform your business in ways you can't predict.

Top talent is harder to come by.
Simple demographics, as well as increasing requirements in positions at all levels, imply that there is greater demand for top talent than there is supply. This means that winning organizations have to search harder for the talent they need and develop new ways to attract and retain it.

Corporate ethics are under increased scrutiny.
Competitive business practices and issues such as privacy, executive compensation, governance, intellectual property, and drug testing have all become headline news in turn.

Security is now a strategic business issue.
Post-9/11 issues of terrorism and global insecurity color almost every business decision. Relocating the corporate headquarters now raises questions of co-location, and phone and IT systems, as well as human safety systems that have to be scrutinized from the perspective of total failure in the event of a terrorist attack.

As Robert Kegan so aptly points out in *In Over Our Heads,*[1] leaders are facing increased orders of magnitude of complexity. As individuals, parents, family members, community members, citizens, professionals, and leaders, we face many issues where there were few before, and they interplay and create unanticipated ripple effects throughout various facets of our lives.

It's the cumulative effect of all these changes acting together that has raised the bar on leadership. As Matt's example shows, you need new skills and a new approach to leadership in order to be able to lead a global corporation today.

All of which raises two important questions that Matt and every other business leader must ask themselves as they navigate their way through these treacherous management waters:

1. What kind of leader do you have to be to deliver results and succeed today?
2. What kind of team do you have to assemble to work with you in this new era?

Before we begin to answer these questions, let's look at a few more examples of the kinds of challenges people are facing today.

Learning Trust

Alyce Cunningham was trying to figure out why Harry was sitting across from her. Was he just the latest person management had sent to check up on her? She was wary, a feeling that had become all too common since her promotion a year ago. She was tired of the second-guessing, frustrated, and wondering if management was just setting her up. "The only reason I'm still here is that my numbers are better than anyone else's," she said to herself grimly, and settled in for what she expected would be yet another tricky conversation.

Twelve months ago, Alyce had been promoted to vice president, operations, Midwest region, for a packaged goods company. She had started almost sixteen years ago in an entry-level position in the procurement department of what was then a small manufacturing company headquartered in Kansas City. Through a series of acquisitions and consolidations, her company now had plants throughout North and South America and, more recently, Asia.

At the time of Alyce's promotion, her company was completing an acquisition that would add seven new manufacturing sites to her region and had decided to consolidate the operations function (procurement, logistics, invoicing, and security) into one centralized function in each region. Although Alyce had worked in each of the areas in Ops, she had never managed a large group or led a consolidation. She was chosen only because her old boss, who was in line for the job, had been unexpectedly recruited to join another company.

Her current boss, Bob, was a senior player who had come up the ranks in manufacturing. Bob put her in the role half expecting her to fail. He viewed her experience and education as weak, but he also knew that he could count on Alyce to get things done and that she was all about the detail. And there was something about her energy and determination he always admired.

Alyce had made it through the first six months in her new position on sheer energy, drive, survival instincts, and long hours. While she wasn't winning popularity contests, her hard work was beginning to pay off. After one year, she had the consolidation behind her, her region had the best performance numbers, and she was making progress putting together a team of direct reports she felt were up to the task.

But Bob was considering replacing her.

Alyce ran a very closed shop and didn't work well with peers in other divisions. The relentless pressure for performance, the company's growing globalization, and recent developments in supply chain management were requiring all of the leadership to be able to coordinate, cooperate, rethink, and work across boundaries and cultures as never before. And Bob was beginning to get complaints about Alyce.

Trying to help her out, he'd given her Brad, a very savvy and senior guy from Manufacturing to head up her strategic planning group. He was hoping Brad could help Alyce fix her growing problems with Manufacturing. And he had brought in someone from Corporate to work with her performance measurement group—in part to audit and in part to help bridge her successes to the rest of the organization.

Alyce had not responded well to these two assignments. She felt they were a sign of mistrust. Instead of listening to them and the rest of her new management team, she felt she needed to be on guard. Their presence made her less willing to explore tough choices with the team, and more concerned about proving she could handle it all.

Bob saw Alyce's potential and believed that if he had the time, he could be a powerful mentor to her. Given the global nature of his responsibilities, though, it was out of the question. He decided to make one more effort before taking drastic action and replacing her.

He asked his admin to find the current number of Harry, a former senior vice president of another manufacturing firm, who had retired five years ago. Bob first met Harry when they were in business school, and they had always hit it off. They had stayed in touch over the years and had recently served on a commission to study some pending regulatory issues. While Harry was enjoying his time off, Bob knew he would sometimes take on special mentoring assignments—if he thought highly enough of the individual and the company.

Alyce has hit the wall of structural trust. Her experience of how trust changes is typical of key leaders.

Outside Thinking Partners Are Too Important to Be Left to Chance

When Jim Corliss moved to London in the 1970s to head the UK business for a multinational company, he was excited about the opportunity and what lay ahead. Although the UK business was currently small, his company believed that this was an area of great potential.

One of the biggest constraints to growth had been a long-standing regulatory environment that made major investments in the UK relatively unattractive. Now, there was a sense in the industry that there was a win-win way to change this environment and that the government would be willing to consider these changes. Jim knew this assignment was a critical one for him. Success would put him squarely in the senior leadership ranks of his company.

When Jim arrived in London, Derek Waddington was already a key player in the company's new lobbying effort within the British government. Derek, Cambridge educated and with a passion for service, had spent the first fifteen years of his career rising to the top of regional government. About ten years ago, Derek decided it was time to step down from government and start a firm focused on bridging government and industry.

After several meetings at which Derek was in attendance, Jim was glad Derek was on the team. There was something about Derek's way of thinking that, while very different from Jim's, was extremely compelling. And Jim had noticed the way Derek skillfully handled a few potentially difficult conversations. Jim realized that Derek was someone of high integrity, possessing much wisdom when it came to navigating complex interpersonal dynamics.

As the months progressed, Jim and Derek found that despite their very different backgrounds, they worked well as a team. Jim had never let anyone challenge his thinking quite the way that Derek did. Derek had opened his eyes to a new, much broader way of thinking about the relationships between business, government, and community, and to a much more nuanced understanding of what it takes to pull off big change. He realized that while working with Derek he had learned to look for the unexpected. And that was sharpening his overall leadership style as well.

Two and a half years later, with a hard-won, major legislative victory in hand, Jim was promoted and returned to the U.S. to head the North American business. It was only back in the U.S., facing a new and very different set of business decisions, that Jim fully realized just how much he had benefited from having Derek, not just as a political operative, but also as a thinking partner. Jim no longer needed Derek's specific expertise in dealing with Parliament, British regulators, and local officials, but he felt the absence of the kind of broad, challenging, and candid inquiry he and Derek had engaged in.

As the flurry of the initial months settled down, Jim realized that without Derek, his leadership was not the same. His current inner circle couldn't provide the kinds of conversations and critical thinking he had come to depend on. Six months into his new position, Jim began to search for a few key people outside the organization with whom he could discuss the wide range of strategic issues facing him in his new assignment.

Most leaders, once they have experienced the benefits of thinking partners, never go back to leading without these kinds of resources on their team. Instead, they continue to look for and develop a broad advisory network throughout their careers.

Today's leaders need to start early and think systematically about the kind of team they want to assemble.

The Role of a Key Leader Demands Rapid Assimilation and Growth

Andy was the kind of key leader every organization looks to have on its management bench. Andy began his career in one of the leading Fortune 100 high-tech companies, excelling in several line and staff roles. Six years ago, he joined a highly regarded professional services firm, where he was widely viewed as an up-and-coming leader. Four of those years he had spent in the field leading casework, and then two years ago he was asked to co-lead an internal team focused on strategy, growth, and organization. In this role, he worked closely with both the president and the CEO.

While he was highly successful at headquarters and learned a great deal from his exposure to the top executives, he realized that he wanted to get back to leading in the trenches. His opportunity for line responsibility came when his firm acquired a midsized creative boutique.

Andy played a key role in the due diligence and deal process, and he developed rapport with the new people. Part of the deal was for the creative firm's current leader to step down. Andy was everyone's choice to step into the role of leading this newly acquired business unit.

Six months into the job, however, things were not going as well as he had hoped. Andy found himself facing increasing challenges.

Pressure from corporate to meet the numbers had accelerated just as the business was facing its first downturn in a decade. The overall market downturn had exposed the boutique's very high cost structure. He had kicked off several initiatives, each under the leadership of one of his key executives, focused on branding, new products, and people. But even these new programs weren't helping the company cope with changing business conditions.

No longer in the center of senior management, Andy was getting confusing signals from the CEO about the long-term strategy for the new acquisition. Inside his new group, Andy felt his every move was being scrutinized. While he had gone the extra mile to get to know people and develop friendly working relationships, he was still the corporate guy, the noncreative outsider.

Andy could see that they were going to have to quickly find a very different way to think about the business. He had hoped for a longer runway of consistent business performance to enable him to really get to know the business and its people. But now he had to take action, and he didn't have time for lots of trial and error.

The combination of challenges Andy faced is not an unusual one for Key Leaders. Young, quickly promoted managers prove themselves at one level only to find that they have to learn a whole new set of competencies at the next.

While each of these cases presents different challenges, they do have several things in common: These leaders are facing more complexity, sooner, and more often, than leaders of the past. They need to lead in areas in which they are not expert. They are regularly confronted with issues that are highly sensitive and need to be handled with great care and sophistication. And, finally, these leaders need expert input and a safe place to ask hard questions where they do not have to constantly filter for spin, self-interest, and other agendas.

What Kind of Advice and Counsel Do Leaders Require Today?

People in high places have always been able to seek advice and counsel from the best and brightest. From the pharaoh's counselors in biblical times, to President John Kennedy and the Cuban missile crisis; from Medieval royal courtiers to Bernard Baruch, Eleanor Roosevelt, and Vernon Jordan; history is full of wise counselors whose primary role was to be a sounding board and intellectual foil for the one in charge.

One of the best known masters of inner-circle advice was Clark Clifford, who during the second half of the twentieth century served as an adviser to several American presidents, most notably John Kennedy and Lyndon Johnson, as well as an adviser to many top corporate leaders. In his memoir, *Counsel to the President,* Clifford describes the vital importance of having well-placed and well-prepared outsiders in a leader's inner circle:

> Even if he ignores the advice, every President should ensure that he gets a third opinion from selected and seasoned private citizens he trusts. (The second opinion should come from Congressional Leaders.) Though Cabinet members and senior White House aides often resent outside advisors, a President takes too many risks when he relies solely on his own staff and the federal bureaucracy for advice. Each has its own personal or institutional priorities to protect. An outside advisor can serve the role of a Doubting Thomas when the bureaucracies

> line up behind a single proposition, or help the President reach a judgment when there is a dispute within the government. They can give the President a different perspective on his own situation; they can be frank with him when White House aides are not.[2]

As should be clear by now, the risks to the organization—and the career—of the individual leader who is determined to go it alone are greater than ever. It is not enough to have a brilliant team of direct reports—what I call your action team—working with you. The history of business in recent years is littered with smart executive teams that didn't see it coming—or if they did, were unable to change the course of the organizational ship in time to do something about it. Leadership in the modern era demands external thinking partners in addition to a top-notch internal team.

As I have worked with leaders at many levels across diverse industries, it has become evident to me that a few talented leaders naturally know how to assemble their advisory network and incorporate it into their leadership team as a powerful and well-utilized resource. But many promising leaders do not.

In the past three years, I've researched the issue intensively, interviewing hundreds of leaders and their advisers and thinking partners in order to understand these issues in depth. This research has lead to two insights that form the heart of this book:

Insight 1: Leadership today requires three new habits: Habit of Mind, Habit of Relationship, and Habit of Focus.

Insight 2: You can start developing the three Habits and your advisory network at any time during your career.

Now we will explore each of these insights in depth.

> *Insight 1:* Leadership today requires three new habits: Habit of Mind, Habit of Relationship, and Habit of Focus. Used together, these Habits will enable you to build a powerful leadership circle and lead with the benefits of outside insight. These Habits are vitally important to what kind of leader you will be. They will distinguish your leadership and your career trajectory.

1. Habit of mind.

Leaders today must master a new level of thinking. I call this *exponential thinking.* Exponential thinking allows you to see all sides of a complex issue; it's the process of examining context, looking for interrelationships, exploring assumptions, and asking questions that reveal the full truth and potential of a situation, like a prism revealing the full spectrum of color within white light. Leadership requires both mastery of exponential thinking and the ability to develop and lead teams of people capable of their own exponential thinking.

As my research reveals, successful leaders need to regularly spend focused time with thinking partners they trust *because exponential thinking is best done with others.* The successful leaders then translate these insights into vision that drives action and results. Exponential thinking plays a particularly important role in decisions where there is high ambiguity, uncertainty, and risk.

Exponential thinking is not really new. Many of the advances of civilization rest on the exponential thinking of great minds. What is new is that exponential thinking is required today for leaders at all levels—and that increasing levels of mastery are required as leaders progress to more and more senior positions. It is a critical leadership capability that we will explore fully in Chapter 3.

2. Habit of relationship.

Leaders today must assemble a new kind of leadership team, one that ensures that they undertake the right kind of exploratory thinking and are challenged by multiple perspectives.

As Figure 1 shows, essentially, this team must be made up of an action team and an inquiry team—which we'll define more thoroughly in Chapter 4—that are capable of translating exponential thinking into useful action. Leaders need external thinking partners on the team so that they can explore sensitive and edgy issues with high trust and external perspective. There is not a fixed, one-to-one correlation between roles and people. One person can, and often does, play different roles (moving, say, from subject expert to thinking partner, and sometimes to action team member) at different times, depending on circumstances, expertise, and interest. Your ability to get results in increasingly boundaryless organizations depends on how well you can orchestrate your network of important relationships.

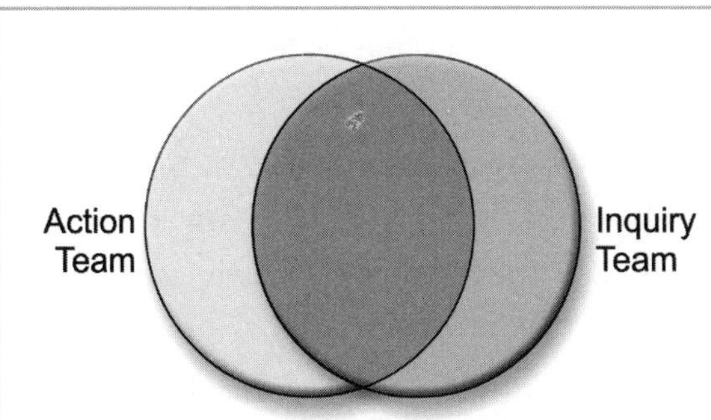

Fig. 1. Leaders must assemble a new kind of leadership team, one that participates in both action and inquiry. A single person can have roles on both teams.

To fully develop your Habit of Relationship, you will need to master different aspects of building trust and understand how your trust in others changes (as does theirs in you) as your career progresses.

Early in their careers, people confront the issue of trust. At first, it's a relatively straightforward matter of developing personal trust—the kind of trust that means you feel comfortable talking in confidence. Or knowing that the people around you will get their jobs done so that you can do yours effectively.

Soon enough, as you rise in the ranks, you will begin to understand the second kind of trust—expertise trust. This is the essential matter of knowing that the advice you're getting is sound. As leaders gain experience, they must become good at making judgments about people's expertise—and doing so quickly and accurately.

Beyond personal trust and expertise trust, there is a third kind of trust—structural trust—and this is the one that often trips up leaders as they take on their first big responsibilities. Structural trust is involved when you've risen to a level above your early career friends and colleagues and your relationships with them shift. They now have agendas or turf to protect—and you can no longer trust them in quite the same way. This is not because your colleagues are bad people or because they wish you ill, but because your position changes the dynamics between you. They want something from you. Or they may have loyalties to other leaders. Or they may be competing with each other (or you) for the same job at the next level.

In short, your relationships are now laced with the self-interest, advocacy, competition, and multiple loyalties that are inherent in organizational life. Now, self-interest in itself in not a problem. Indeed, it often is a powerful force for good. The problem comes when leaders fail to understand that the input they're getting is limited or biased—or, conversely, they sense the limits and, in response, retreat from even second-opinion conversations, becoming further isolated in their thinking.

Structural trust concerns raise a key question: how do other people's current or future roles affect their relationship to you? In light of their responsibility to their roles, their organizations, or their own careers, are they structurally able (vs. personally able or willing) to be fully loyal to you? Having a relationship of highest structural trust means that there is no doubt in your mind that the people you choose as your thinking partners do not have, and will never have, an agenda that competes with your own. Building the right leadership circle means that you will need to develop the ability to seek out and attract people of high personal, expertise, and structural trust to your inner circle. Without these resources, you will be left with a critical hole in your leadership team.

3. Habit of focus.

Leaders must have the skill and discipline to focus on the essential non-urgent issues. Today, leaders are faced with information overload and ever-increasing demands for speed. In this environment, more and more daily work has become urgent. But just getting the daily work done is not what your leadership is about. Leaders must be able to create and execute strategies to carry out their leadership agendas. They must be able to use their inquiry teams and advisory network to get this critical work done right.

Mastery of the Habit of Focus—that is, to function effectively in your high-pressure environment and make progress on the big, longer-term issues that still need your attention—is required of all leaders. Your sustained focus on the non-urgent important issues defines the core of your leadership; it is what ultimately differentiates your unique contributions and your ability to deliver value no one else can. Your Habit of Focus is what gets results, distinguishes you, and builds your career.

Developed over a lifetime of leadership, these three Habits, like all good habits, become part of your character and are a source of strength in trying times.

> *Insight 2:* You can start developing the three Habits and your advisory network at any time during your career. It's important to develop and use the three Habits in concert. While everyone will use them differently, there are guidelines to help you focus on perfecting the various parts of each habit as your leadership progresses.

Where do today's business leaders turn for outside insight to help them navigate the leadership terrain successfully? Each leader's sources will be different. For you, it will probably be a mix of formal and informal networks. For John Brown, managing partner at a worldwide recruitment firm, the key to outside insight is an informal network of fellow executives who have gotten together on a regular basis for years. One member of the group is a consulting partner John met in business school. Another runs a CEO consulting practice. One manages investments, and another is a contrarian marketing genius known for consistently offering what John calls "bundles of ideas, three of which are completely insane, but one of which is always a total 'Ah hah!'"

According to Brown, "Some people might just want to pick your brain. In our group, everyone brings ideas and issues and topics. We make sure that the benefit flows in all directions."

There is a range of models for developing a properly balanced advisory network, and they vary depending on your career level.

Most likely, you already have some sort of advisory network, though it may not be developed to its potential or well tuned to your current leadership challenges.

In Chapters 7, 8, and 9, we will fully explore the practical steps to creating the unique network of resources that is best for you. We will discuss the development and use of the most important parts of each of the three Habits as your career progresses from Early to Key to Senior Leadership. You will develop a full understanding of the resources, tools, and networks you have at your disposal. And you will learn a set of sequential steps and questions to ask yourself that will serve as your road map for the journey.

Important Inner-Circle Conversations

Conversations with inner-circle thinking partners are broad ranging and typically fall into one or more of four basic categories.

1. The visionary conversation.

The primary purpose of this kind of dialogue is to imagine the different possible futures that one might create, and use that insight in the present. In this kind of conversation, you and your thinking partners consider world trends—micro- and macroeconomics, global and political realities, scientific and technological developments—sometimes as much as seven to ten years into the future. If this is the future you want to commit to creating (or to avoiding), what are the steps you should take now to influence the desired outcome?

2. The sounding board conversation.

This conversation takes place when you want to work with someone who has the right expertise, wisdom, and experience to take a third-opinion look at a new strategy or a set of ideas. You and your thinking partner look together at the implicit assumptions involved in the course of action, check them against external reality, and vet the decision in a variety of ways, including legal, political, and environmental implications. You want to ask the "what-and-why" questions. ("What if we looked at it this way?" "Why do we believe that this is right?" "What's the sacred cow that we might not be willing to touch?")

In leadership, the little things need to go right as well as the big things. The sounding board conversation is the place to explore actions and decisions of all sizes and importance, as well as to explore doubts and, perhaps, to discover the wisdom behind the doubts. It is a place to explore certainty and to find the limits of that certainty.

3. The big picture conversation.
In this conversation, a leader and a thinking partner step back and look at all the things that are going on, making sure that where you intend to go is aligned with all the complex and interdependent moving parts involved in getting there. The purpose is to make sure that nothing has been left out, that your thinking hasn't become blinkered by a too-narrow corporate focus.

4. The "expertise in inquiry" conversation.
In these dialogues, the leader is looking for more than an expert problem-solving conversation. You are looking not only to develop your knowledge, but also to develop fundamental models and new ways of thinking about the terrain. You need a thinking partner who is an expert, an expansive thinker, and someone who can help you learn the new information in ways that are highly relevant to your current situation.

The leadership terrain is complex, and the thinking required to master that terrain is concomitantly demanding. Thus, learning what you are *not* a master of is just as important as developing your thinking skills. To be a successful leader today you need, perhaps above all, to know your own limits. And then you need to know how to go out and find others who can take you the rest of the way.

By this point you may be wondering, Is this book a book about executive coaching? No, and yes. Within this broader discussion of advisers and thinking partners, where does the executive coach fit in? Probably the best way to think about it is this: executive coaches are one species within the genus of thinking partner. While there is no one definition of exactly what an executive coach is, typically they are a highly specialized group with expertise in inter- and intrapersonal dynamics, communications, and, often, organizational development. The top executive coaches typically work as thinking partners with their clients on issues in these areas. In addition, they often explore areas of personal leadership, thinking with leaders about their purpose and authenticity.

The rapid development of executive coaching points to the more general need leaders have for entirely confidential, external thinking partners to help them explore the issues with which they are confronted. What's often lost sight of is the inherent limitation in the types of business issues that executive coaches can help with. Given their expertise and resulting bias toward human dynamics, you need to be highly cautious in turning to your executive coach for exponential thinking on, say, business strategy. Would you turn to a psychologist when who you really need is a Jack Welch?

What Do You Look for in Your Most Important Advisers and Thinking Partners?

Thinking partners are exponential thinkers who are able to offer you new information and new lines of sight. They explore existing mental models and work with others to challenge and expand their own mental models. They are skilled at looking for hidden assumptions, in testing and validating, and in challenging the status quo. They are appropriately wary of thinking by analogy.

The best thinking partners have a well-developed ability to think across parochial boundaries. They have an aptitude for detecting interdependencies and they know how, fundamentally, to see a problem at several different levels—and have the ability to pick the right level for the best solution.

The capabilities of your inner-circle thinking partners should reach well beyond categories of expertise, such as finance, global strategy, product development, or organizational dynamics. In short, here's what you look for:

- The ability to see all sides of a complex issue (exponential thinking).
- Someone who asks great questions and listens closely—including for what isn't said.
- Someone who doesn't offer advice.
- Someone who has a reputation for integrity.
- Someone who has high-quality expertise and experience relevant to the key issues you need to resolve.
- A person who can provide unique perspective.

- Someone who has the ability to tailor content to challenges and questions at hand.
- Someone who clicks with you intellectually as well as personally.
- Someone who has an intuitive understanding of your strengths and meshes well with them.
- A person who possesses authentic curiosity and empathy.
- Someone who is free from conflict of interest, both personal and structural.
- Someone who reciprocates in choosing you.

It's hard to imagine leaders who would not want to have people like this on their team. It's powerful, interesting, fun, and a safety net, all at the same time. Beyond that, it's deeply satisfying to build and sustain these kinds of lifelong leadership relationships.

It's Unique to You

Your inner-circle advisers and thinking partners are the most unique and personal part of your network and leadership team. There is no substitute for the leadership work of seeking the third opinion and incorporating outside insight. You have no obligation to work with anyone not of your choosing. And there are no set formulas. How you develop and call upon your network of relationships can and should reflect your style and what's best about your leadership.

The remaining chapters of this book provide you with the path and the tools to build your lifelong network and full leadership circle. You can start at any time. The rewards are well worth the effort.

CHAPTER 2

The Three Habits

When we left Matt Whalen in Chapter 1, he was reaching for the phone. As you'll recall, he was dealing with a difficult question: should he disclose the financial maneuver his company had been involved in before the press gets wind of it? It's not a given that the press ever will hear of the move his company made. The company has done nothing wrong. But the press can easily take something like an aggressive financial transaction such as this one and turn it into a caricature of bad corporate behavior. The downside risk is considerable. Because Matt is a good leader, he'll also want to think about the upside potential in this situation. Is there any way to turn this corporate sow's ear into a silk purse?

To get to the answer, Matt will need to integrate his understanding of certain possible tactics with his expert knowledge about the business he's in and its concomitant financial risks and rewards. And he'll need to apply some hard thinking—what I call exponential thinking—to the problem. He'll have to rely on his **Habit of Mind.**

Matt is reaching for the phone because he knows he shouldn't think alone about his problem. He realizes that he needs a third opinion. Throughout his career, Matt has taken care to bring some trusted outside advisers into his inner circle of thinking partners. He's done this because he's realized that there would be certain things he wouldn't be able to discuss with his colleagues or direct reports. There would be times when he needed to bounce ideas off of disinterested parties who nonetheless know Matt and his company and can quickly get up to speed on the current situation. For such a network to exist, it has to be cultivated in anticipation of events like this. You can't create it in the moment of crisis, for obvious reasons of trust and familiarity. This means that you have to cultivate your **Habit of Relationship.**

Finally, besides being able to recognize that this issue must be addressed immediately, Matt needs to be able to push away the urgent things on his agenda today in order to deal with it. The ability to deal with the many items on your plate and still carve out time for surprises is what I call the **Habit of Focus.** You must be able to distinguish between the essential and the merely urgent and know how much time to allot to each.

Back to Matt.

First, he calls Charles, a partner in a local law firm that Matt knows well and has retained many times as outside counsel. Matt wants Charles to personally take a second look at the financial and legal analyses regarding this transaction. He asks Charles to bring in whomever he wants on the finance side—he trusts Charles and wants him to work with someone he's comfortable with.

Next he talks to Kevin. Kevin is a friend dating back to business school and a manager at a PR agency. He has a good read on how the press will react.

Charles's initial read is as Matt expected. He agrees with Matt's assessment that there appear to be no illegal actions or improper accounting. He and his colleague will take some time to check all the details, but that is the likely conclusion. He also thinks that given the technical nature of the issue and the fact that nothing improper occurred, it is highly unlikely that the press will pick it up.

Kevin, on the other hand, expresses much more concern about the press. Of course, Kevin has seen it all, and he knows that the press sells copy with catchy headlines—and he can see an angle that would drag Matt's firm into the thick of things. Kevin thinks there might be some ways to beat them to the punch, but he makes sure that Matt knows that he cannot trust the press to see things from his perspective, give him a fair and impartial hearing, or present all the relevant facts. Kevin encourages Matt to fire up the entire corporate PR team (Matt's company does not use Kevin's firm, so no conflict of interest exists) to get ahead of this potential PR explosion.

In addition to Charles and Kevin, Matt has called me. We begin by reviewing what's known, and then look at the situation from all perspectives. One of the first things we notice is that the facts on the outside are few, and the possible outcomes we could make up to fit these facts vary widely. We draw a range of these, looking for key assumptions that drive different outcomes.

Eventually, it became clear that, far from making a dumb mistake, Matt's firm had in fact done a reasonable thing. Matt realizes that he has on his hands a great story about highly ethical success at the company, not a scandal.

Matt and I keep going back and forth—I'm not there to provide the expert answer, but to act as a sounding board, challenging all aspects of the thinking and making sure we've left no stone unturned. We come up with a lot of ideas, but we keep coming back to the fact that while Matt cannot control the actions of the press, he must have a way to turn the situation to his advantage.

Instead of spending a lot of time arguing the merits of particular actions with the highly unpredictable press, we look for strategies others have used when faced with situations they could not control.

The "Ah hah!" moment comes when we think about how fire fighters fight fire with fire—when it crosses certain thresholds.

If the press picks up on the situation and starts the blaze of a negative story, Matt could be ready to go with a bigger, more encompassing and revealing story that would surround, engulf, and change the direction of the initial story. His story would reveal more and show what went right, not wrong, when his company made the initial investment. Instead of trying to use friends and contacts to kill the story, if (and only if) he had to, he'd use every friend and contact he had to fan the flames, fighting fire with fire, and, in so doing, influence the direction and impact of the story.

Now, the action plan falls into place. Matt's best and most trusted speechwriter and a team of internal people get to work on drafting the story, getting the contact lists in order, and getting Matt fully prepped if the story does break.

Some executives would have stopped there. But Matt and I push onward. How did this potentially explosive situation happen? What should be done differently? With the immediate plan now in place, what is the best way for Matt to inform and ready the firm, just in case?

What happened? The press didn't pick up the story. Matt didn't have to fight fire with fire. He did use the story written for the press to get the right conversations happening within his firm. Shortly after the crisis had passed, these conversations led to adding the topic of perception risk to internal quarterly risk reviews. This made all the difference when an issue of ethics came up in South America six months later that the press did get wind of.

Matt was given high marks by his superiors for the way he handled the crisis. His people also gave him high marks. Rather than trying to find someone to blame, he made it clear that he still supported risk taking and created a way for them to safely discuss risk and give early warnings.

Habit of Mind, Habit of Relationship, Habit of Focus—all three work together to help you anticipate, evaluate, and decide on a course of action that not only avoids potential disaster, but also creates new intellectual and social capital for the company and better prepares it for the future.

How much time have you spent developing these habits, consciously or unconsciously? Think about your current leadership circles and ask yourself:

- What kind of network have I built, and how and when do I use it?
- Are there teachers, mentors, friends, and activities that have been particularly important in my development at some stage in my life?
- How do I include my spouse or significant other, family members, and personal friends in my current leadership circles?
- When have I had a conversation or ongoing dialogue where I significantly changed my understanding or learned something I did not expect? What were the conditions that led to the insight?
- Are there critical areas for me now where I have no thinking partner, or where the thinking partners I have are lacking in expertise, perspective, or appropriate structural trust?

CHAPTER 3

Habit of Mind

Succeeding at the leadership level today—where people like Matt, Alyce, Jim, and Andy operate—requires a new Habit of Mind, meaning that you have cultivated the ability to think and lead in a high-speed world of change and interdependencies. There are three facets to this Habit of Mind: *mastery of three levels of thinking, curiosity and self-knowledge,* and *spotting great talent for your inquiry team.*

MASTERY OF THREE LEVELS OF THINKING

Leaders today must extend their abilities to integrate new and old information, plan more flexibly, and be ready to redefine the very way they understand their job, company, and marketplace. In order to accomplish this, leaders must develop mastery in three basic types of thinking: *application, expert,* and *exponential.* I will take each of these in turn, but a key point to keep in mind as we proceed is that it is *in the integration of all three kinds of thinking* that leaders will find their ability to successfully deliver results over time.

Application Thinking: Mapping the *Known* onto the *Unknown*

Application thinking is focused on planning and implementing well-understood methods in ways that yield replicable results. People skilled in application thinking can readily identify the characteristics of a problem and, with the benefit of experience and history, find a solution. Application thinking consumes the greatest share of most managers' mental energy. While there may be substantial innovation and variation in this recombination of existing solutions, the intent of application thinking is to generate consistent results through familiar methods.

Expert Thinking: Invoking Deep Understanding of a Specific Subject

Expert thinking begins with people who have developed deep understanding and expertise in specific fields of knowledge, such as markets, technologies, disciplines, or theoretical constructs. In business, expert thinking is brought to bear when challenges and issues are new or unique and don't fit easily into a solution by a known method. In many cases these issues have a highly technical component (e.g., finance, legal, economics, operations, technology, science, human dynamics). Approaching the issue from their area of specialty, expert thinkers bring new perspective to diagnosis, and the technical knowledge and problem-solving abilities to develop custom approaches and solutions.

Expert thinking can provide alternate potential solutions to problems, along with analysis of the strengths and weaknesses of various approaches. It often brings with it access to a network of related experts whose own thinking may be brought to bear on various parts of the problem. Of course, expert thinking and application thinking are interrelated.

Exponential Thinking: Exploring New Terrain with New Frameworks

Exponential thinking, as we've already discussed, is the work of developing multidimensional framing that helps leaders see all sides of a complex issue in ways that yield insight about the nature of the complexity at hand. This kind of thinking is the most difficult to master, so we will devote the most attention to it. Until you master exponential thinking, you won't be able to take full advantage of the third opinion.

While the intent of application thinking is replicable results, and the intent of expert thinking is innovative and customized solutions, the purpose of exponential thinking is to achieve insight. The starting point for expert thinking is building on what is known, and the starting point for exponential thinking is curiosity about what is unknown and about unexplored relationships. This means that *inherent in the nature of exponential thinking is the need to engage with others who bring different perspectives and who are capable of helping you to explore issues outside of your awareness, mental models, and current understanding.*

Exponential thinking contains two key elements: first, expertise in one or more fields of knowledge, and, second, the capacity to apply that expertise to explore interdependencies, make sense of multiple perspectives, unearth and validate assumptions, and envision possible futures in ways that yield new ideas and insights.

An underlying characteristic of exponential thinking is that insight shifts occur when problems are reframed and then explored at a higher level of context and complexity. As a very simple example, if you are running an assembly line and one of your machines keeps breaking down, you can focus on the machine as the problem, and set about fixing it as quickly as possible. However, if you reframe the problem at one higher level of systems complexity, you will see how the machine is a part of an overall assembly line and thus connected to other machines. It might be revealed that the problem machine is breaking because other machines are sending it components too fast, and the permanent fix might be to retune the timing of the line rather than repeated repairs of the problem machine. Donald Schön and Chris Argyris, writing in the 1970s, named this basic shift in thinking "double loop learning."[1]

In today's world, we are faced with multiple levels of potentially interdependent "double loops." Economics forms a loop with geopolitical realities. Markets loop with structural realignment, with discontinuities in science and technology, and with regulatory and oversight changes. Work-force issues loop with breakthroughs in communication infrastructure. Globalization requires loops of sophisticated and subtle understanding of local issues, culture, and use of language. Inclusiveness comes with loops of historical context and diverse perspective. Broad, big-picture agendas loop with individual emotional intelligence.[2] Every leader faces these kinds of interdependent loops. The successful ones know how to embrace them and find the connections.

The Six Steps for Exponential Thinking

1. Understand the mental models that guide your thinking.

What are the mental models that govern your thinking? At the level of your business, your mental models are made up of assumptions about how your business works. These include the marketplaces your company sells in, the key levers of change in those marketplaces, and the nature of your competition. Beyond that, you have more fundamental assumptions about the world and your place in it.

Our mental models deeply impact how we make sense of things and also how we choose to act.[3] They develop from individual experience and from our cultural and intellectual heritages. Although human beings may share universal perceptions of primitive environmental stimuli, certain cognitive patterns, and the ability to generalize new uses of language from existing patterns, we understand reality in highly individual ways. As Karen Otazo points out in *Executive Coaching,* "We unconsciously filter the world through our own paradigms or worldviews and believe that what we see is the only reality. . . . Because we think ours is the only reality, other perspectives may appear irrational, naïve, or misguided."[4]

Thus, the starting point for exponential thinking is to develop an awareness of our mental models and those of others.

2. Develop your ability to discern patterns.

Our ability to see and recognize patterns is one of the fundamental human sense-making capabilities. As leaders, we need to look for patterns all the time and practice spotting them in different situations and in a variety of contexts.

Particularly, the ability to recognize when a new element cannot be fitted into an existing pattern, but must form the beginning of a new pattern, is an essential modern business leadership skill. As we expand our repertoire of different possible mental models, we expand our ability to see patterns in more than one way.

3. Check and recheck for hidden assumptions.

Much of what we do on a day-to-day basis is guided by assumptions we hold—for example, about markets, customers, competition, talent, ethics, and the like. A key part of exponential thinking is unearthing and examining our own assumptions and how they affect our thinking.

There are many tools that can help you unearth assumptions about your business. For example, Six Sigma[5] is a method that enables you to increase operational results and quality in sustainable ways. Part of the power of this kind of tool is that it uses a structured approach to move from operational conjecture to measurable fact, revealing hidden assumptions. For a broader set of business problems, the Ladder of Inference,[6] first explored by Chris Argyris, can help you unearth and validate the assumptions beneath your points of view. And finally, Charles Hampden-Turner's recent work on culture[7] is one tool among many that will help you understand the cross-cultural assumptions and challenges in your business today.

4. Create varied scenarios of the future.

The exponential thinker considers mental models, patterns, and assumptions and uses them to develop a portfolio of scenarios for the future, like a good chess player who combines pattern recognition and risk assessment to work five, seven, even ten moves ahead. The exponential thinker has the ability and judgment to create multiple views of the future, compare one to another, determine their relative probabilities, and commit to a course of action that allows for the ability to switch if and when needed.

The dark side of action is the law of unintended consequences. Disk drive developers who relentlessly increased the sophistication and functional capacity of their products unwittingly created a new market for competitors at the low end when their ability to make technological innovation outstripped the customers' ability to assimilate it.[8] By taking the long view, the exponential thinker can plant seeds for future opportunities, even in the face of great change.[9]

5. Look for ways to broaden your line of sight.

It is a truism today that we live in a deluge of information and data, so the last thing we want is more vying for our attention. In fact, everyone is looking for ways to get more value from less.

But to develop the necessary Habit of Mind for successful leadership today means that you have to think very carefully about how you get your information, its sources, and its sources' sources. Because information comes at us so fast and in such volume, we don't typically take the time to parse the data and consider its reliability. Small-scale health studies, to take one example, are often picked up in the press, simplified, and overstated, and then become gospel before researchers are able to confirm the results with any certainty. The outcome is that we risk basing personal health decisions on outdated, incomplete, or distorted information.

Most information that reaches us has been filtered for perspective and spin. The danger for leaders in large companies as they become more senior is that they often move into such a rarefied information environment that all the information they receive—especially that which is labeled "privileged and confidential"—is filtered through the same few channels.

When they become too isolated, leaders lose their awareness of the strategies, norms, beliefs, and agendas of anyone besides their own teams. In the worst cases, such isolation can facilitate purposeful obfuscation, undetected errors, and costly cover-ups.

Winston Churchill was so acutely aware of this problem, made worse by the way in which his fame and charisma intimidated staff, that he set up a separate, side bureaucracy—one not reporting to him—to provide a purer channel of information. Ensuring diversity of your sources is part of the job.

As a leader, it is your responsibility to question the source of the information you receive—especially the information that you rely on most unconsciously and take most for granted. How often and how systematically do you ask yourself, What are the needs of the groups or individuals supplying this information? Why have they made it available to me? How would I act on this information if I knew that it was reliable? How would I act if I knew that it was not? Do I need to plan scenarios based on these possibilities?

Expert advisers in a particular field often have what I call "line of sight"—that is, they have deep knowledge about a field and early access to information and events—before some of this information is widely known. For this reason, these experts can spot trends long before they become apparent to the average citizen.

Leaders need to have their own lines of sight. They need to understand the limits of those lines of sight. And they need to develop relationships with others that give them a portfolio of lines of sight—much broader than they can create on their own. What does your expertise allow you to see? What knowledge does it close off to you? Knowing what you don't know is as important in an information-saturated era as knowledge itself.

6. Invest in your ability to think in the gray space. The higher you progress through the leadership ranks, the more your role is to take your organization where it has never gone before. But, like a journalist writing daily dispatches, creating the rough draft of history, leaders on the cutting edge have no established references to sort out the big picture for them. It is the leader's job to be the first to *discover* that new reality—to push the boundaries of what's known, what's acceptable, what's comfortable, what's legal, what's practical. That is, to lead in a land where things are not clear and delineated but, rather, fuzzy, unpredictable—in a word, gray.

What do you do when faced with decisions that require you to use judgment in the face of the unknown? Developing your ability to lead in the gray spaces starts first with simply strengthening your awareness of when and where you are in the gray zones. It's ambiguous, but how ambiguous? It's inconsistent, but how inconsistent? It's edgy and untested, but how edgy? How varied are the different interpretations of fact? How much does a little variance in one area impact the entire outcome? How many plausible stories could you create? Beyond asking yourself these questions, there are some practical steps you can take to improve your thinking in shades of gray.

Consider the case of Gary McNeill. When Gary left his position as a senior partner in a prestigious consulting firm to take over as COO and SVP of strategic decisions at Holder United, he knew his primary challenge was to restructure Holder's portfolio to get the stock valuation going up again.

As he probed, cut, and reshaped Holder United, he was looking not just for incremental growth, but for big wins. In the process, he noticed an intriguing anomaly. One of Holder's companies was

SwiftProducts, which sold propellant into the transportation industry. Nonetheless, a small but significant percentage of SwiftProducts's sales were going to pharmaceutical houses. Gary did a little digging and discovered that these customers were using the propellant in clinical trials for drug delivery systems for AIDS and flu vaccines. Not only was this an area with compelling opportunities for growth, it was also an area of real human need.

But could it be the basis for a solid business, a focused business that could consistently meet both performance goals and regulatory scrutiny? Perhaps, but was Holder United a reasonable place to build such a business? Holder was already spread too thin in too many disparate fields. It had no experience in the regulatory environment of pharmaceuticals. And healthcare was about as far from its concentration in smokestack industries as any business could be.

Like most leaders, Gary had a long list of business opportunities to consider, and he was prepared to let this one go, as simply too long a shot for Holder. But something wouldn't allow him to let it go. Here was a chance to significantly improve the lives of literally millions of human beings, and that thought just wouldn't let Gary alone.

Facing many unknowns, Gary asked himself, first, if there was one issue that could make or break this idea. *Is the underlying technology sound enough to base an entire business on? Is the scientific discovery phase really over, or are there hidden technical issues that will crop up?*

Then, to proceed, what would he next have to assume that, if it turned out to be false, would stop the show? *What manufacturing requirements are necessary to succeed in this business and regulatory environment, and how likely are we to be able to meet them, and in what time frame? How hard is it, as a new player, to meet the requirements for the necessary approvals? Is this realistic, and how would I know?*

Finally, *what would I need to know about the kind of talent required to build and run a company like this, and what would I have to believe about our ability to attract and retain this kind of team?*

Gary knew he didn't have the necessary expertise to explore the potential of this project on his own. He didn't want his internal team, a great source for second opinions, distracted—and he was afraid that it would not have a fresh enough perspective. So Gary turned to external advisers and thinking partners to help launch a business that ultimately proved to be very important indeed.

First, he retained an outside top scientist, Christopher, to vet the pharmacological aspects of the underlying science and teach Gary enough about the science so that he could actually understand and frame the most important technical considerations.

On the basis of the technical vetting, as well as his own growing confidence with the science, Gary began searching for a thinking partner with serious experience in the pharmacological industry, someone with the requisite network, with manufacturing expertise, and with solid grounding in regulatory procedures. Working through his own highly developed network, Gary found just the right person, Xian.

After they had thoroughly framed and explored the issue of manufacturing and regulatory requirements without hitting a barrier, Gary sought the advice and expertise of a longtime HR colleague, Hubert. Hubert and Gary worked on the culture required to attract and retain the right talent.

By the time he was ready to make a significant investment in this project, he had developed with these three thinking partners a clear point of view, a solid framework for a plan, and several ways to anticipate and deal with potential resistance and doubt from Holder insiders.

The new business got off to a fast start. Early on, the technical adviser, Christopher, was a big asset. His reputation as a lead scientist on several blockbuster products preceded him and gave the new venture instant credibility within the technical groups. Christopher's participation and reputation helped Gary to recruit Charlotte, a well-qualified general manager from the pharmaceutical industry (and a big win for Gary)—and once in place, Christopher became the key technical adviser for Charlotte. And he was still available to Gary if the need arose. In addition, Christopher chaired the scientific advisory board for the firm, enabling Holder to bring in a group of scientists who would not otherwise have been accessible or interested.

Xian, on the other hand, remained primarily an outside thinking partner and a powerful source of third opinions for Gary, helping him look at how this new venture was developing and how Corporate needed to support—not smother—the new venture, and brokering important regulatory relationships. With so many other operating issues on Gary's plate, Xian helped him stay up to speed with the venture and keep focused on the issues that would support longer-term success.

Charlotte had her own network and soon brought in Joan, a strategic thinking partner she had worked with over the years. Xian and Joan found ways to meet regularly, which helped keep Charlotte and Gary in synch. As Charlotte set out to build the leadership team, develop the plan, and get the venture moving, she used a combination of hiring and sourcing outside experts, some of whom performed specific tasks on a limited basis and some of whom later joined the company.

Bottom line: Gary's initial investment of $40 million to develop this line turned into a business worth $500 million a year. The products turned out to be safe, with very high efficacy for AIDS medicines and flu vaccines. They were cost effective and highly profitable. Under Gary's guidance, Holder United learned how to build and sustain a very different kind of business that had synergy in the portfolio. And the new business had a real impact on the lives of countless individuals.

Gary's method of thinking backward from the desired outcome might be called "thinking in the gray space 101."[10]

Thinking backward may be insufficient to reach a decision when the stakes are very high, and the future cannot be anticipated with any real precision. A more advanced level of working in the gray space is to lead from a portfolio of options. When each of the options has its own ambiguities and potential downside, none is the obvious winner, and a choice must be made, you must consider your own strengths and those of your team. Which option are you best prepared to follow through on? Which downside can you best survive? Which one generates the most passion?

Finally, if you have exhausted these means of evaluation and still have no clear outcome, and yet you must make a decision, then consider the quality of your thinking and perspective on the subject. How much work has gone into these solutions? How intensely have you felt the various possible outcomes and scenarios? What worst-case risks are too big to absorb? These are the questions to pose yourself before making your best intuitive decision.

CURIOSITY AND SELF-KNOWLEDGE

To lead in today's corporations, it is essential to have a realistic picture of yourself. This is especially true as you develop thinking partners and pursue exponential thinking. The kind of realistic self-assessment we're talking about here is not necessarily self-knowledge in any deeply philosophical sense, but simply an accurate picture of how you function best within your organization.

Develop Your Curiosity

A good leader is a curious leader. Sometimes it's hard to explore all the areas that strike your interest when you are under pressure to perform, but it's vital that you make time to engage your natural curiosity.

Curious leaders possess a self-confidence that allows them to remain open and inquisitive, even in the face of sometimes being wrong. They are deeply aware of context, of the convergence of circumstances that creates challenges and opportunities. This supports their habit of questioning "givens" and looking for new ways to test assumptions.

Curious leaders want to know more than just how to get something done. They thrive on understanding underlying principles and on comprehending where and when these principles apply (or don't). While able to acknowledge success, they are as deeply interested in what didn't work as they are in what did. They regularly inquire into their own ignorance, looking for their blind spots, and always work to push the boundaries of their knowledge. Curiosity needs guidance and sustenance. In great leaders, relentless curiosity is deeply linked to a commitment to something bigger than themselves and bigger than their current circumstances.

Understand Your Managerial Style

We all have natural preferences in our ways of working—what work we gravitate toward, what kinds of environments we like, how we like to think. From early in your career, you will have developed your work styles, and it is incumbent upon you to notice them, to understand how well they work for you—and when they don't work so well. Ask yourself, How do I fill up my time—in face-to-face meetings or in solo work? How do I feel at the end of the day, when I have spent time with people or alone? Which energizes me? What kind of environment do I like to have around me? Do I need chaos and energy or quiet purposeful activity? These sorts of questions need to be answered regularly in a kind of self-audit.

A simple and useful tool for discovering your managerial style is to fill in Figure 2 (page 48). The columns represent three perspectives through which leaders tend to look at issues, and the rows represent functional areas. (Of course, these need to be adjusted to your work—for example, if you are a divisional finance executive, your functional areas might be strategy, risk, financial structure, HR, compliance, systems, tax, and investments.) Each box represents an area where an organizational problem might arise—for example, a technical problem in marketing or a relational problem in operations (e.g., relationships with suppliers, labor, etc.). Think about the kinds of problems you prefer or the ones you tend to work

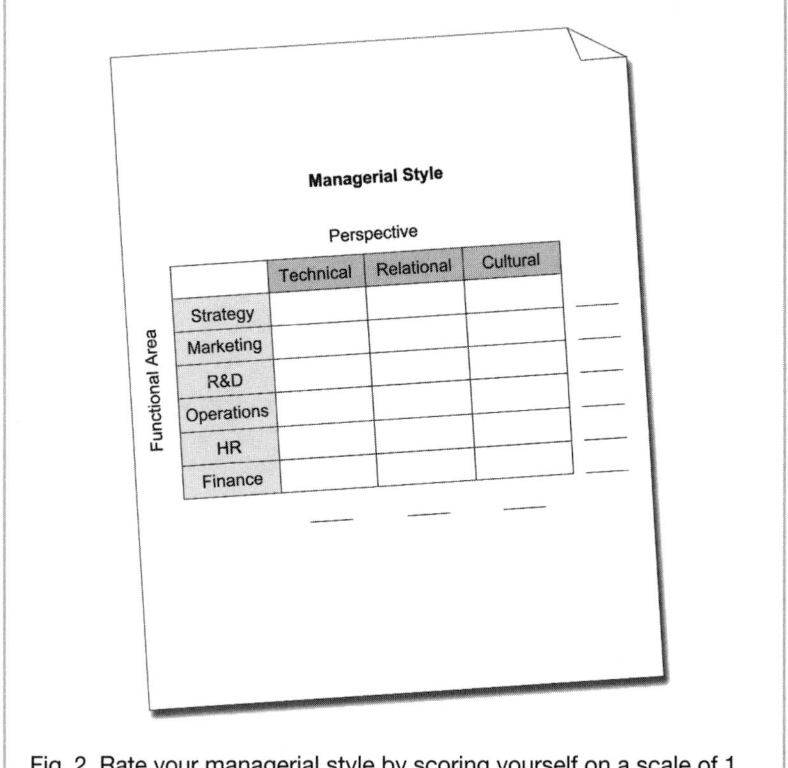

Managerial Style

Perspective

Functional Area

	Technical	Relational	Cultural
Strategy			
Marketing			
R&D			
Operations			
HR			
Finance			

Fig. 2. Rate your managerial style by scoring yourself on a scale of 1 (least prefer) to 10 (most prefer).

on first. Put in a 10 for the ones you prefer the most, and a 1 for the ones you least prefer. Summing rows and columns gives you a better idea of your managerial style.[11]

The distribution of your column scores indicates your preferred leadership perspective. The low and high row scores indicate your preferences for challenges in different functional areas.

Understanding your own managerial style is, of course, a way of analyzing your own biases and mental models, so you can question whether your natural biases and strengths are positively or negatively affecting your approach to certain issues.

Be Aware of Your Style of Thinking with Others

Some managers like debating with colleagues who hold strongly opposed views in order to find the potential flaws in each. Others prefer discourse, starting with an outlined situation and exploring all the facets. Still others are much more intuitive, preferring to listen to a discussion and, after evaluating everyone else's opinions, following their gut instincts. Knowing your own style well will allow you to complement that style with others in your inner circle. It will allow you to understand the kinds of problems that you won't be able to manage as well as others so that you'll more quickly know when you need to ask for a third opinion.

How Do You Process Information?

In some companies people are expected to present written briefs as a primary method of communication. In others, written briefs may rarely be used, but presentations are considered ineffective without PowerPoint demonstrations or other visuals.

What works best for you? Do you learn visually, or do you need to have a conversation to sort out your options before making a decision? Do you understand interrelationships best when they are represented spatially or when you experience them kinesthetically? It's your responsibility to ensure that you get your information in the format that you can integrate best, but also that you work to develop your other capacities for processing information, because sometimes you can't control the way in which important information is presented to you.[12]

Don't Believe Your Own Hype

We now have a twenty-four-hour news cycle and an always-hungry press. Leaders are featured in the press at much earlier stages in their careers than they were in the past. In a networked organization, personal press is part of scooping the competition. But remember that press is about spin. As personal marketing becomes a larger part of professional life, you need to be careful. Personal press and personal branding are important, but they're antithetical to exponential thinking and the Habit of Mind—especially if they go to your head or you begin to believe your own publicity.

SPOTTING GREAT TALENT FOR YOUR INQUIRY TEAM

As important as it is for you to be aware of your styles, strengths, and capabilities, it is equally important for you to develop an ability to evaluate others and their strengths, weaknesses, preferences, and biases. Much has been written about the need for this skill when building great action teams.[13] But it is just as important in building a leadership circle.

Know the Difference between Advisers and Thinking Partners

In addition to clearly articulating the importance and role of outside advisers, Clark Clifford makes a distinction that is crucial to understanding what is required in inner-circle inquiry for leaders today, exemplified in his years of service to two very different presidents:

> The relationship I had with each man [Kennedy, Johnson] was quite different. When Kennedy called on me, it was usually to play a clearly defined role on a specific problem—from the aftermath of the Bay of Pigs to the Steel Crisis. Johnson, on the other hand, wanted my advice or observations on almost anything that might confront him. . . . Johnson . . . asked me to participate in important national security meetings which otherwise involved only government officials, something Kennedy never did. In these meetings, I would say little unless asked to comment by the President—and even then I shared my views with him later, only in private.[14]

Clifford's description captures the essential distinction between two important but different advisory roles: that of the adviser and that of the thinking partner.

President Kennedy turned to Clifford mainly as an adviser, calling upon him as an expert to engage primarily in expert thinking. Clifford proposed alternatives and solutions to Kennedy's tough domestic and international political problems.

For President Johnson, Clifford's role took on quite different dimensions, combining expert thinking with the broader realm of exponential thinking. Seeking expertise including international law, diplomacy, defense, and issues of national security, Johnson would ask Clifford to take on advisory assignments to read and research materials, report back on critical issues, and help him to find specific alternatives and solutions to tough problems. At other times, Johnson would ask Clifford to think through issues with him, looking for strengths and weaknesses. In this role, Clifford's expertise and his mastery of exponential thinking enabled him to ask insightful questions. At still other times, Johnson would ask Clifford to be an observer rather than a direct participant. Clifford became a reflective foil and a trusted sounding board for open-ended, and exceedingly private, exploration of the interconnectedness of the issues. This is the role of the thinking partner—the third opinion.

Distinguishing between the roles of adviser and thinking partner helps you develop the advisory network that is most relevant to you and your leadership challenges. As you think about it, you will notice that there are people who may be superb advisory resources who are not as talented in the thinking partner realm. To cultivate the right leadership inner circle for you, you will want to hone your ability to make this distinction. In Chapters 7, 8, and 9, we will explore tools and guidelines that are designed for each stage of your leadership. You will find that these distinctions will help you figure out what kind of thinking needs to be done, and will help you clarify the range of resources you need on your inquiry team.

Emulate Those You Admire Most

To develop your own Habit of Mind, it is important to understand how other leaders develop themselves and their thinking. There is no one right way. Do the leaders you admire have an inner circle for inquiry that supports their development? If they are any good, they surely do. Is there something you can learn by understanding how top sports figures choose coaches and trainers? What does Bill Gates do to push his thinking? How about Jack Welch? How did his inner inquiry circle work? What can you learn from the leaders around you? What makes it possible for the leaders you admire most to continue to grow—no matter how famous they are, or how insightful, or how often right?

Be curious. Study these leaders and learn from them. Other leaders' examples are perhaps the best way for you to leapfrog the usual mistakes. There are many examples that can and should guide and inspire your thinking. While inner-circle conversations are quite private, once you begin to look for them, there is much about a leader's network of advice and counsel that is accessible and worth thinking about. This is lifelong learning—it's never too early to begin seeking to understand how outside insight has served those you admire most.

In summary, what is required of the leadership mind today? First, you must develop mastery in exponential thinking. You must keep your curiosity alive. You must know yourself and develop a strong ability to think in the gray space. Finally, you must learn from and be inspired by other leaders and their thinking partners, who together continuously raise the bar on their collective thinking capacity. This is the Habit of Mind of a successful leader.

CHAPTER 4

Habit of Relationship

Remember Alyce Cunningham from Chapter 1? As you'll recall, Alyce had come up through Ops to a leadership position. Her boss, Bob, saw that she was committed and tough and that she could consistently get results in her areas of functional expertise. But she didn't have the skills for more general leadership, and that deficiency was starting to get in the way of both her career and the company's performance. Bob wasn't sure if Alyce could make the transition to her new role. But he wanted to give her the chance. He asked Harry, a retired SVP of manufacturing from another firm, to consider working with her as a thinking partner.

Bob starts by asking her to meet with Harry regarding the new industrywide subcommittee on security he's heading, explaining that working with him will give her more of the external exposure she needs.

Alyce wonders, Am I being set up or is this for real?

To her surprise, Alyce finds Harry easy to talk to. There's something about the way that Harry's mind works—the way he frames interesting questions—that she finds intriguing. Without taking any credit, he gives her several useful ideas in their first meeting, and he seems to be learning from her as well. Harry tells her about his industry committee and about his work with key leaders who are looking for a sounding board or mentor.

Alyce finds herself outlining the main components of her security program. Harry asks tough questions about risk and trade-offs. She finds she's grateful for this conversation; it's quite different to push these gray-area questions around with someone who has no agenda or stake in the outcome.

She comments on this.

"Right," Harry says. "It is different. That's what draws me to do this kind of work. Leaders must have great action teams—I always invested in mine to the max—but they also need people who are external and disinterested to explore sensitive issues and uncertainties. Otherwise they become too isolated."

Common sense, but she'd never quite thought about it that way before. Not until much later that evening does Alyce realize that Harry has put his finger on one of the things she likes the least about her new position: with power and responsibility comes isolation. Everyone around her now has an agenda. She invites him to come back and spend a day with her to think about security and risk. Several members of her team are also pleased—they're excited about the external exposure they are getting and looking forward to meeting Harry.

Thus Harry begins working with Alyce as an expert on security, but soon he's something more: her sounding board for her nonurgent, yet important agenda—the third opinion. Immersed in tough-minded thinking sessions with Harry on a range of topics, Alyce discovers that she is good at thinking about things from a large-systems perspective. And there's more.

Working with Harry, Alyce begins to realize the difference between allies and confidants. This breaks a logjam for her. She begins to look at how to create allies and not expect them to be more. She begins to look for ways of working with others that respect differences of agenda, but are win–win.

For instance, Alyce is able to change her relationship with Brad, the savvy and senior guy from Manufacturing whom Bob had brought in to head up her strategic planning group. Instead of seeing him as a threat, she unlocks the potential of his second opinion and finds he has enormous energy and expertise. While he has limits to his structural trust, inside those limits he is genuinely interested in helping her to be successful. With Brad's help she is even able to bring a colleague from Manufacturing into her circle—someone she had previously treated with skepticism because she could see no further than his vested interests. Finally, Harry persuades Alyce to bring in an executive coach to help her develop a more sophisticated worldview and presence. Working with the executive coach, Alyce starts to have better results from those cross-regional meetings.

The rest of the story? Alyce's hard work has paid off. The firm is reorganizing into three regions, with Bob as global head of operations. He has created a global head of strategic projects and asked Alyce to take the position. By wrestling with the issues of trust that had held her back, Alyce has been able to work with Harry to grow as a leader. Moreover, her increasingly sophisticated understanding of trust and leadership has enabled her to broaden her network of advisers and thinking partners. Now, she can more effectively engage a wide range of people, internally and externally, in a way that shifts her performance to a higher level of achievement and makes her stronger.

Alyce has started down the path of learning how to develop the **Habit of Relationship.**

The Habit of Relationship Begins with Relationship to Self

You need to understand how you work with team members and thinking partners—your Habit of Relationship—to ensure that you undertake the right kind of thinking—your Habit of Mind—on the important issues.

In fully engaged exponential thinking with others, you

- Listen.
- Are willing to be wrong.
- Ask for help.
- Create an environment in which people feel safe expressing opinions.
- Share the spotlight.
- Know when to do expert and exponential thinking.
- Think about yourself as part of a larger whole—or many larger wholes.
- Are committed to developing your own capacity and that of others.

Think about it. How many times have you worked with leaders who you felt really didn't listen, never admitted being wrong, or took all the credit? How likely were they to miss things, have others not tell them important information, or find themselves unwittingly out on a limb on some issue? How often did you feel such leaders were committed to developing the best in their team and in themselves?

Now, look at yourself. What rankings would you give yourself on the preceding points? When and how do your habits affect your ability to do exponential thinking when it really matters, to draw the best exponential thinkers to you, and to have people with the courage and commitment to speak the unvarnished truth? When and how do these habits create opportunities for you to fail?

Knowing yourself—your gifts and your faults—is the starting point. The next step is to build relationships that support and sustain your leadership—with trust. Trust is dynamic, not static. There are lots of good reasons to build a high-trust company and culture—but that doesn't mean that the same levels of trust apply to everyone. How fully can you trust in situations of overlapping cooperation and competition? In situations where there are winners and losers, and the stakes are high? Trust is an issue that leaders must regularly revisit. It is perhaps the central question of leadership, because leaders must work through others to achieve their goals. And to work through others and know that the work is getting done, you must have a well-developed ability to cultivate and build relationships along all the dimensions of trust.

Understanding Trust

My research reveals three fundamental distinctions of trust that leaders must understand and develop: personal trust, expertise trust, and structural trust.

Personal Trust

Leaders in the early stages of their careers can easily understand the first and most basic kind of trust, personal trust. This is the trust that develops in the workplace from shared tasks and an understanding of what makes your colleagues tick. Once you've been with them working late to meet a deadline, or responding to an emergency on a shop floor, you begin to know, and trust, what they are made of. For most people, this is the basic meaning of trust. It is knowing that your team mates won't let you down, and vice versa, when it counts.

This sort of understanding is encompassed by the simple question, "On a personal level, do I trust this person?"—meaning, do I believe that this person is basically honest and ethical? Do I believe that he will make good when he gives his word? Do I believe that this person is basically well intentioned? Do I believe that this person will handle confidential information with care and discretion?

But it is precisely this understanding of trust that gets leaders into trouble later on in their careers. The team that proved so ready to help when you were one of them has a differen agenda, suddenly, now that you are head of the division. They come to you looking for two things: the same old trust and something new—access to power and influence that comes from your new position.

Instinctively, you realize you can no longer trust them in the same way that you did before. You may not be able to fully articulate what's different, but you know something is. And you start to behave differently.

Two new kinds of trust that go beyond personal trust now become important. You must be clear about them, because failure to understand them will trap leaders and end careers before they have a chance to soar.

Expertise Trust

First, there is expertise trust, the trust that comes from competence and knowledge in a particular subject matter or process. You've had enough experience with your marketing colleague to know that she has a world-class mind for thinking strategically about markets and segmentation, but you've also seen her make organizational decisions that give you pause in speaking with her about much of anything outside of her expert realm.

More important, you shouldn't. Trust works both ways, and, as a business unit leader, you can't discuss with her the implications of an impending reorganization—to do so would be a breach of a different kind of trust called structural trust. More about that in a moment.

Expertise trust focuses on the knowledge, judgment, and thinking abilities of someone else. "Do I trust that these people are expert in their fields? That their knowledge is current and up-to-date? Do I trust the information they gather to inform and support their positions? Their ability to understand my situation and apply their knowledge to it? Their judgment regarding risk, options, and trade-offs? Their ability to innovate and develop custom solutions to hard problems? Their ability to do exponential thinking? That they will know and tell me when they don't know?"

These are the sorts of questions to ask about people's expertise. As you rise through the ranks, you will need to be able to discern quickly to what degree you can trust the expertise of the people you run across—regardless of the level of personal trust you might establish with them. These aspects of trust have points of intersection. Of course, if you find someone completely untrustworthy on a personal level, that's a different story.

Structural Trust

Structural trust refers to how much someone's position or role affects your confidence that he will be able to deal with you straightforwardly. "Are such people in roles where their judgment and thinking is likely to be significantly influenced by their need to advance their goals, self-interest, or advocacy? In light of their roles, are they structurally able (vs. personally able or willing) to be fully loyal to me? Where might they have competing sets of loyalties? Are these people in roles where they are likely to filter data and input to me? Does the nature of their roles make it is unwise for them to be fully honest and direct with me? On some issues? On all issues? Are they likely to move into roles in the future where there will be structural constraints to our level of trust? (For example, will we be competing for the same position or for the same client some day?)"

This is the kind of trust that changes the most as you become more senior. In most companies, at the entry level, you have relatively little reason to be concerned with structural trust, but as you move into higher positions, increasingly the people you encounter will want to influence your thinking for their own purposes. Or they will want to spin the information you see to support their goals and metrics. Or they will want to sell you something. Or they will be highly competitive and will exploit signs of vulnerability.

In short, your relationships are interlaced with self-interest, advocacy and, at best, multiple loyalties, of which loyalty to you is only one. This in and of itself is not a bad thing—you want teams and people where advocacy, self-interest, and action line up. Self-interest, mitigated by the right kind of governance, is a highly positive force in innovation and exploration. The problem is that many leaders either don't understand the dynamics at play or don't know how to translate this knowledge to work in their best interest—or both.

Many leaders don't fully understand that while you can and should work with people with whom you share medium levels of structural trust, you must have some people in your inner circle with whom you share the highest levels of structural trust—as well as high personal and expertise trust.

The absence of high structural trust relationships is a critical hole in your leadership team.

Leaders Must Think Systematically about the Nature of Their Relationships

The nature of your relationships becomes much more complex as you rise through the leadership ranks. It is never too early to begin to think systematically about your work teams, advisers, experts, and friends.

First, we need to explore three different categories of relationships: action vs. inquiry, internal vs. external, and working vs. inner circles.

To create balanced and powerful leadership, begin by developing your action and inquiry teams. You will need, of course, action teams to carry out the day-to-day business of the organization you now lead. You will need to fight fires, solve problems, set goals, meet contingencies, and so on down the list. Beyond that you will need teams of inquiry—teams that help you think beyond what's urgent and immediate to what's important and long-lasting, teams that think with you about strategy, direction, focus, sustained growth, the nature of the marketplaces now and in the future, and the like.

Obviously, in your networks of relationships, action and inquiry will not always be independent realms. Leadership at all levels requires agility in working with many of the same people in both modes, intertwining inquiry with action to drive results and performance.

You also need to build your internal and external circles, creating connection between the world of your organization and the world outside.

Exponential thinking, done properly, means balancing action and inquiry, and working with both internal and external people.

Exponential thinking is, by its very nature, a matter of crossing intellectual boundaries. You can't do the whole job when confined to the internal world of your organization. You can't do the whole job without regularly thinking about unfiltered (or differently filtered) information. You can't do the whole job without looking for hidden or habitual assumptions, without vetting key ideas with people not invested in the perspective and culture of your organization.

It should be emphasized, however, that developing powerful resources in your external network is not about offsetting weak teams or covering for other organizational deficiencies. In fact, the better your internal teams are, the better your external teams need to be, so they can help you find the leverage that's outside traditional organizational boundaries and put it to use. That's how you build a business culture that embraces new ideas, constantly raises the bar, invites collaboration, and is positioned for flexibility.

Leaders Need to Balance Internal and External, Inner- and Working-Circle Relationships

Thirty to forty years ago, a leader's external network wasn't complicated. Typically, it was populated by old friends and by the traditional professional services: legal counsel, financial advisers, and investment bankers.

Over the last twenty to thirty years, newer professional services, including management, technology, and infrastructure consulting, joined these ranks. These professionals typically provide highly skilled resources that can augment the capacities of your teams.

In the past ten years, the leadership territory has expanded to include an even wider range of external people. Today your work necessarily crosses boundaries with customers and supply chain. There are alliance and joint venture partners as well as licensees, industry-wide standards committees with whom you must work closely, and regulatory bodies.

Thus today you are working with many more external people on action. You therefore need to expand your external teams for inquiry in a similar way. Indeed, you need to integrate all four networks to increase the flow of performance back to the action team, the team charged with getting measurable results.

So whom exactly do you recruit for each network?

Contacts Are the People at the Edges of Your Networks

Contacts are the people who make up your extended network, the people who are in your Palm Pilot or database of contacts. They are generally casual acquaintances, people you are in touch with from time to time. Everyone knows that contacts are an invaluable resource, and we would be hard pressed to find someone who has reached the senior executive ranks who is not well networked. But for many executives, even those with a well-developed and loyal contact base, their network is focused on their action teams, both internal and external.

In *The Tipping Point,* Malcolm Gladwell makes the very simple but powerful case for the value of even the most seemingly remote contacts. He notes that people who are natural "connectors," those who instinctively build large, diverse networks, intuitively understand the strength of what sociologist Mark Granovetter calls "weak ties," the link to people at the edges of networks. The value of contacts is that they "by definition occupy a very different world than you." And therein lies their simple power for inquiry: "They are much more likely to know something you don't."[1] It's crucial that you develop a varied and robust group of contacts for your inquiry teams.

Your working circle is the essence of your daily work life; your inner circle is increasingly important as you rise through the ranks.

Your working circle is made up of the people you are regularly in

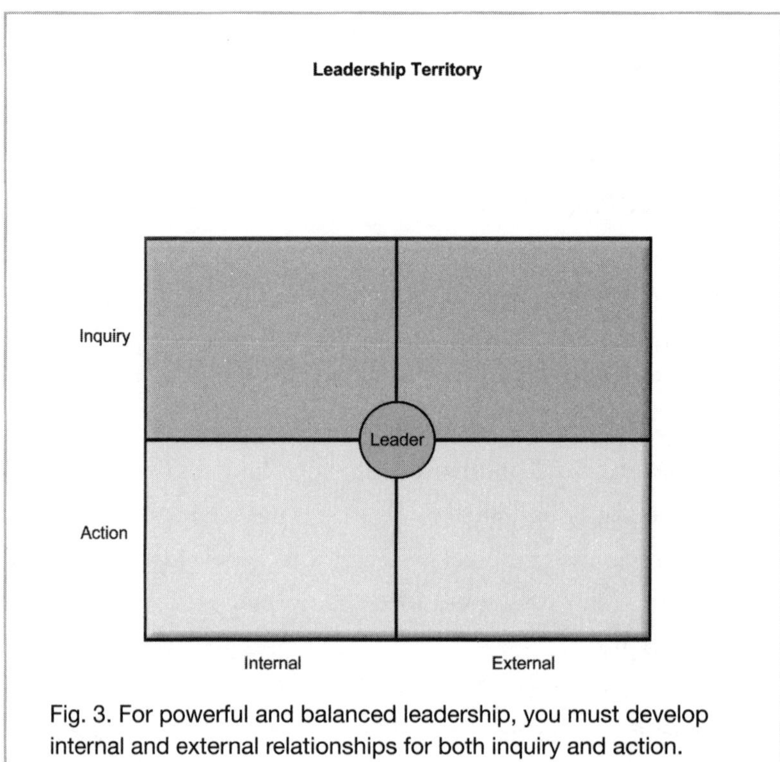

Fig. 3. For powerful and balanced leadership, you must develop internal and external relationships for both inquiry and action.

contact with and count on as resources. The distinction between working circle and inner circle takes on greater significance as one progresses from Early Leader to Key Leader to Senior Leader.

For Early Leaders (Figure 4), the distinction is not particularly meaningful in a structural sense, but as you start to have responsibility over people who also have significant managerial roles, your inner circle begins to come into focus (Figure 5, page 68). Your inner circle will likely include key staff members, your boss, your team leaders, and possibly other colleagues with whom you work intensively.

As you move to the ranks of Key and Senior Leadership, with broad responsibility for large divisions, resources, and results, the

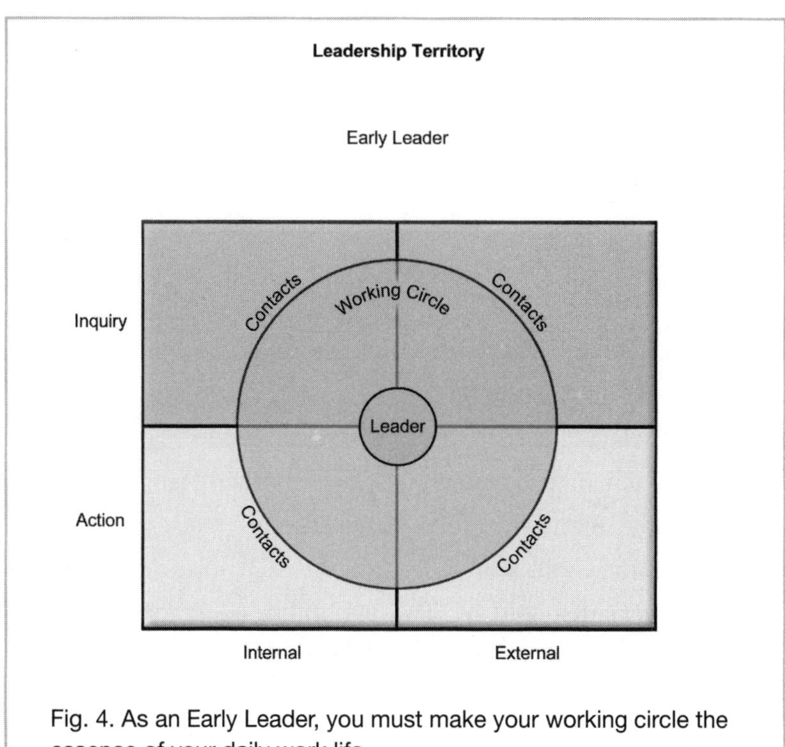

Fig. 4. As an Early Leader, you must make your working circle the essence of your daily work life.

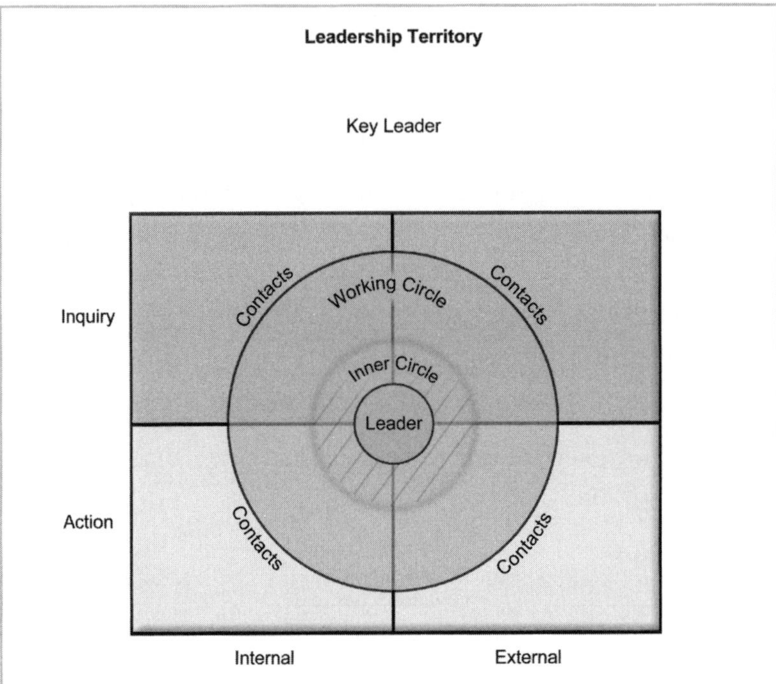

Fig. 5. As you move through the ranks to Key Leader, you will begin to see distinctions between your working circle and your inner circle.

distinction between inner and working circles becomes even more important. Being clear about the distinction allows you to focus, to effectively delegate, and to leverage your time. (See Figure 6.)

You look for high personal and expertise trust on your inquiry teams. In your inquiry working circles, you are likely to find many members with whom you have only medium levels of structural trust. This is as it should be. This is because working-circle members often have roles that have inherent structural tensions with your role. But this doesn't mean that the working-circle people are not as important as inner-circle people—indeed, their positions will

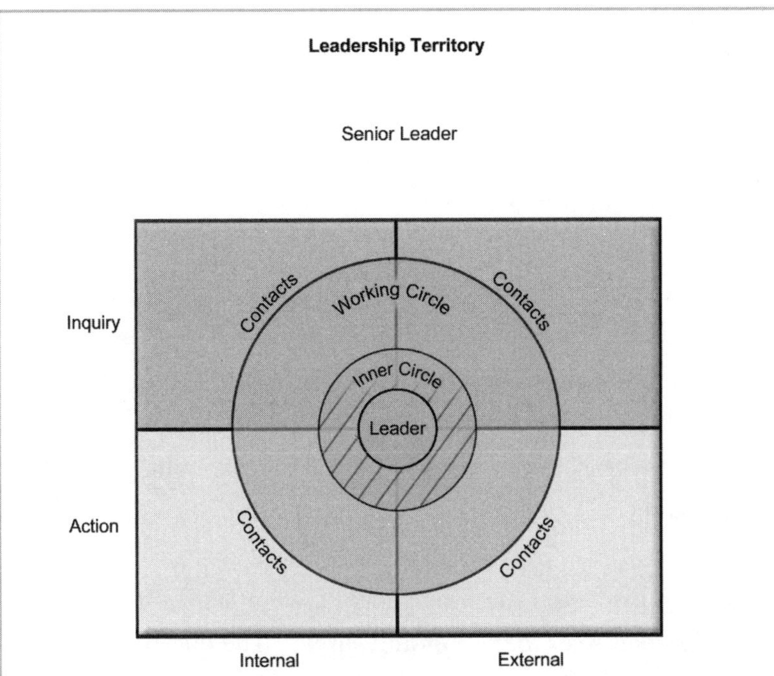

Fig. 6. As a Senior Leader, you will find the distinction between your inner and working circles much clearer. You need to develop your inner circle so that you can share the highest personal, expertise, and structural trust.

often allow them to give you highly useful counsel, in carefully chosen areas of inquiry. As you bring people into your inner circle of inquiry, you need to be sure that in addition to high personal and expertise trust, you have high structural trust. You need both. *But never mistake a working-circle inquiry team member for an inner-circle inquiry team member.* The former quite possibly has conflicting loyalties. At best, his own agenda will color his advice and, at worst, he may even betray you when given the opportunity. It is a dangerous mistake to treat someone as a full-fledged confidant when structural considerations indicate that at best he should be welcomed as an ally.[2]

If you don't cultivate powerful relationships with people with whom you have high personal, expertise, and structural trust, you will make one of two mistakes:

- You will know there are issues where it's unsafe to talk to your team, so you will go it alone—leaving you underpowered and your leadership vulnerable (and often, over time, unsatisfying).
- You'll talk about issues where it's structurally unsafe and get "killed."

In most cases, you want the people in your action/inner circle to play important roles in your inquiry circles. The question is where? *You want to foster extensive overlap between your action inner circle and inquiry working circle.* This may seem at first glance to be a counterintuitive finding. Don't the people in your action inner circle belong in your inquiry inner circle? The answer is no, not always, because the inquiry inner circle requires a higher level of structural trust than the action inner circle does. Medium structural trust is required of both action inner-circle and inquiry working-circle members. Only the inquiry inner circle requires high structural trust.

As a rule, the overlap between your action inner circle and your inquiry inner circle will be small, and those who appear in both should be carefully selected. Jack Welch, in *Straight from the Gut,* talks about the importance of "business soul mates," that is, the internal leaders from his inquiry working circles who make it into his inquiry inner circle.[3]

The same issue of structural trust applies to your external circles. The selection process in choosing who from your external action teams can be brought into external inquiry working circles, or even into your external inquiry inner circle, is worth careful consideration.

The Third Opinion Balances Your Entire Inner Circle

The external-inquiry inner circle is the key balance point for the inner circle of your leadership territory when viewed as a whole. External-inquiry inner-circle team members are the most personal part of your advisory network and are also where you have the most choice. Here alone, there is no obligation to work with the resource pool provided by the organization. While exponential thinking can occur anywhere, it is your external-inquiry inner circle that holds the greatest potential for uniquely powerful perspectives, freedom, trust, and wisdom. You turn to these people for your important third opinions.

The people you choose to join you in this inner circle of thinking partners have to be committed to and capable of functioning without conflict of interests or divided loyalty. You also need access to people who are your peers (or better). By "peer," I do not mean that CEOs should talk only to CEOs and so on down the line. What counts is range of experience, ability, and judgment.

Effective and responsible leadership at times demands that you first learn privately, if only to find the right questions. On certain highly charged issues, you will need to prepare for the group's emotional reactions. At other times, it might be your own emotional intensity or uncertainty that needs to be addressed and dispensed with before you lead meaningful inquiry with the group.

On many issues it isn't primarily a matter of emotional charge—some people simply can't learn in groups until they are ready. And once you expose an issue to open discussion, quantum effects enter in, ripples and feedback loops that distort any further examination. An external-inquiry inner circle can provide the necessary sanctuary for protecting inquiry from the pressures of group dynamics.

What if the head of a business unit begins to consider exiting the core business? Over time, such leaders need to think deeply about the consequences, engaging with their inner and working circles. But once they engage in discussion with teams whose lives will be affected by these deliberations, events are set in motion that will affect the outcome. This means there is work to do before the discussion begins. The leader needs to have done the right preparatory thinking and have an effective sounding board in place. Without an external-inquiry inner-circle team, the leader is left to consider the issues alone, or to engage with other team members who are not disinterested parties. The external-inquiry inner circle allows you to think the unthinkable in complete confidence, without fear of inadvertently setting events, and an avalanche of reactions, in motion before you are ready.

This need to avoid unintended consequences is why people become more isolated as they take on greater responsibility. As we've noted, the more senior you become, the greater the number of barriers that make you less able to speak and think spontaneously. But isolation limits your effectiveness, leaving you trying to manage complexity without the resources you need.

As a leader, you are alone in the responsibility to make the final decisions and live with the consequences—this comes with the territory. But you don't have to be isolated in your thinking. In fact, the greater your responsibilities, the more imperative it is that you talk with others. The solution to both problems—executive isolation and inhibited inquiry—is a well-populated external-inquiry inner circle.

Ultimately, this team contains the people with whom you can

and must expand the edge of your own comfort zone by exploring the unvarnished truth. Accordingly, you want them to be thinking partners who will push you, who have the ability and willingness to ask, not just the unasked questions, but, when needed, the "unaskable" questions. They also must have the ability to look for and recognize the possibility of unintended consequences.

Four Signs That It's Time to Reach for the Third Opinion

Over the years, as I have listened to leaders talk about their most successful work with their external-inquiry inner circle, patterns have emerged about how and when they knew it was time to reach to the inner circle. You will likely recognize some of these:

1. "I'm capable of this, but I just don't have time to think about all of it with the right amount of focus."
2. "If I don't get this right, we'll be in serious trouble."
3. "Even if I had the time, I shouldn't take on these issues alone."
4. "I can handle this, but how might I accelerate or enable significantly better results if I thought through my options with someone else?"

Trust and perspective have never been more critical for leaders. The development of your inquiry inner circle is lifelong and evolving. It's never too late to start, and it does look very different at different stages of your career. Trust takes time; it cannot be created instantly, it cannot be coerced, and it cannot be bought.

CHAPTER 5

Habit of Focus

As Juan Jimenez leaves his office to hop a plane to the coast, his assistant catches him and falls into a fast walk beside him. She hands him a lengthy-looking list. It's all the people who have asked for a piece of his time. "Don't commit to anything before you check with me," she says. "I'm already booking you into April."

"But it's only January 6!" Juan exclaims, shaking his head. He's energized after a week off for the holidays, and he's looking forward to the coming year. But how's he going to get his calendar under control? His division had some spectacular year-end productivity numbers, and one of the major research investments he bet on two years ago just returned some very promising trial data. Could be a blockbuster in another few years. No wonder everyone's after him.

Juan is senior vice president of the second largest R&D division in his company, a major multinational pharmaceutical powerhouse. Over the holidays, Juan had the chance to step back from the action and think about the big things he'd like to accomplish this year. He wanted to schedule a day-long meeting to start thinking about one of the big ideas. But when he looked for a good time to put the meeting on his calendar, he realized that 65 to 70 percent of his time was committed to day-to-day stuff that he just had to do. There's the U.S. executive committee meeting and, shortly after that, the global R&D executive meeting. Budgets, research reviews, research investment committee meetings, research area strategy meetings, hiring, promotions—the list is long and growing longer.

Juan's calendar is more typical of leaders today than not. Leaders at all levels often start their year with the majority of their time already "mandated" to the regular, day-to-day work of their job. This means that leaders typically are left with at best 30-something percent of their time to devote to leadership that reaches beyond the day-to-day.

The hardest part of leadership is to keep sustained focus on what is essential, not just what is urgent. What will create new advantage? What discontinuous change is coming to the marketplace? What are the highest-priority competitive threats? When Stephen Covey wrote his *Seven Habits of Highly Effective People,*[1] he pointed out that if too much of your work is urgent, you are not appropriately focused on what's important; thus you just careen from crisis to crisis. Feel familiar? Because of the avalanche of e-mail, voicemail, information overload, and ever increasing demand for speed, more and more daily work has become urgent. Faced with this reality, mastering the Habit of Focus—the ability to move forward with important but non-urgent issues in a chaotic, high-pressure environment—is crucial to effective leadership. This sustained focus on the non-urgent yet important issues defines your unique contributions to your company and your ability to deliver value no one else can. And, of course, your ability to create value is what ultimately drives your career.[2]

This means that you must devote your most precious resource—*your unscheduled time*—to the most important issues, the ones that hold the greatest potential to yield the highest returns over time. This includes systematic reflection on your overall use of this precious resource. Where is your market headed? What are your competitors preparing for you? How might new market entrants overturn the existing realities?

Using your time for reflection and inquiry is harder to do than it might look at first glance. The great gravitational force of the workday gives immediate tasks too much pull. Without careful planning, you will find your time constantly slipping away in the tug of the diurnal.

You are responsible for your focus. Your boss, your position, your circumstances—each of these may define a significant part of your focus, but not all. You need to be very thoughtful about how you maintain your focus on important results and creating the highest value.

How many times have you been (or seen someone else be) very focused, working long hours to reach a difficult result, only to find out that by the time it has been achieved, it's no longer relevant?

If you intend to focus on some important issue that reaches beyond urgent, day-to-day matters, you need to make it a real part of your work. You need to schedule time, space, and resources, or it won't happen. Urgent issues have huge pull and will take up all your time and then some if you let them.

The Habit of Focus uses your Habit of Mind and Habit of Relationship to drive results from your non-urgent, yet important, leadership agenda.

Framing Issues Clearly and Strategically Is the Work of Leadership

To begin developing a Habit of Focus, you have to frame your agenda. Strategically framing issues—setting context, time frame, scope, and viewpoint—is work that is among the cornerstones of leadership.

But you shouldn't do it alone—in fact, quite the opposite. You should work with your best thinkers and with considerable input from your full inner circle. Why? Because framing work is inherently exponential. How you frame guides what you can see—what models you are choosing, what assumptions, what interrelationships, and so on.

Here are some key things to think about when framing your agenda:

- How narrow or broadly am I thinking about my challenges?
- Would it be helpful to frame the key issues at several different levels?
- What is my time frame for this issue? Why?
- Where does this issue fall in terms of importance and priority?
- What mental models and assumptions do I have that could affect how I frame this issue?
- What tools might I use to frame this issue and what are the limits of these tools?
- Finally, what's known and not known about this issue?

Of course, beyond framing specific issues, you need to have a clear sense of what your overall leadership challenge looks like. Only once you have a sense of the whole can you develop a reasoned response to any particular issue.

Focus Your Leadership Inquiry with the Star of Complexity Map™

I have developed a technique I call the Star of Complexity Map that supports and guides your Habit of Focus. This tool allows you to map and prioritize the issues you think about in inquiry, and helps you focus your time, exponential resources, and thinking partners on the right issues.

The Star of Complexity Map enables you to take an integrated look at all the intersecting opportunities, challenges, and responsibilities you face—your entire leadership mandate. It helps you to see the sets of issues and the types of conversations that are getting the least attention, and where a change of focus could offer the most benefit. It is a thinking tool that helps you ask questions such as the following: What else is there? Are there fresher ways of looking at the problems? What is it that, left untested, could blindside me later? What is it that, if fully explored with someone else, might truly improve my leadership abilities?

The Star of Complexity Map looks at where you are supported or limited by expertise, exponential thinking, line of sight, and structural trust. This allows you to see where you have strong and weak second opinions, and where getting the third opinion is most important. The Star of Complexity Map is designed to help you reflect on how you might best achieve the full benefit of your full advisory network—advisers, thinking partners, and other resources—in all aspects of your enterprise, gaining the right balance of trust, perspective, and expertise at critical junctures.

To explore how you can use this tool, let's return to Andy, whom we first met in Chapter 1. As you'll recall, Andy had jumped at the chance to lead a boutique professional services firm his company had acquired. Six months into the job, however, things were not going as well as he had hoped.

No longer at HQ, Andy was getting confusing signals from the CEO about the long-term strategy for the new acquisition. Andy felt that his every move was being scrutinized. While he had gone the extra mile to get to know people and to develop friendly working relationships, he was still the corporate guy, the noncreative outsider. He and his new management team shared most key assumptions about what drove the business, but he could also see that, given the new economic realities, they were all going to have to find a very different way to think about those driving forces. He had hoped for a longer period of consistent business performance to enable him to really get to know the business and its people. But now he had to take action.

When Andy called to ask if I would help him think through some of the dilemmas he was facing, I suggested there might be several possible conversations we could pursue. He and I had worked together before, when I had served as an adviser and thinking partner to one of the senior executives at his previous company. I suggested that we begin by diagramming his Star of Complexity Map. To begin this process, we needed to put on paper all the critical issues in his leadership mandate.

I asked Andy to start with the following questions:

- What are all the key business issues that you are focused on?
- What do you need to consider most?
- What issues are going to have the most significant impact?

Andy gave these questions some thought, then came back with a list that looked like this:

- Strategic positioning.
- Revenue: pipeline, backlog, and client relationships.
- New sources of revenue: new offerings, IP rationalization, innovation.

- Talent. (It's critical to the business, and managing "creatives" is different.)
- Profitability/cost structure.
- Changing corporate investment/metrics.
- Synergy with other business units.

In testing the list for completeness, I asked Andy to take a look at the six categories of business issues in Figure 7 to see if he had covered all of them.

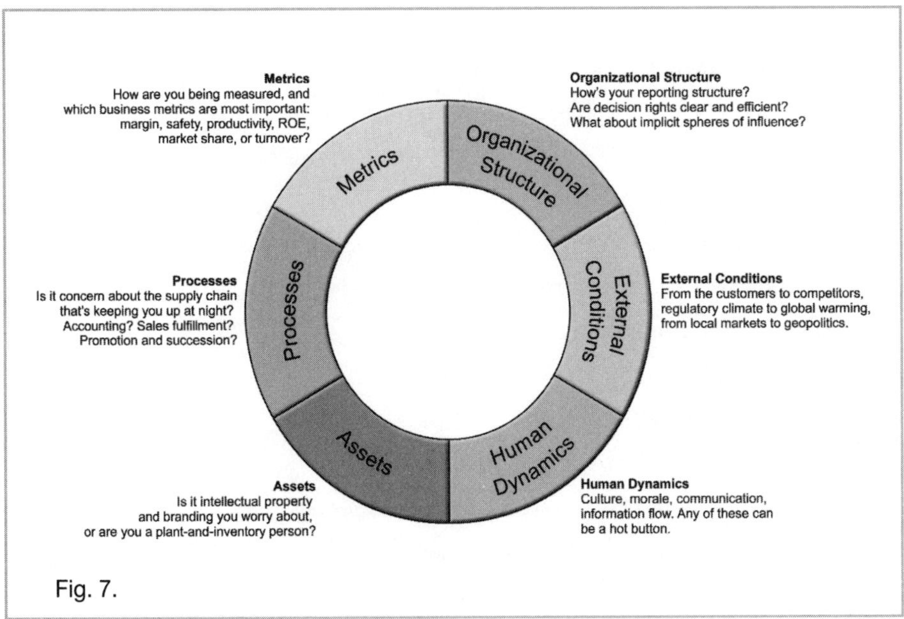

Metrics
How are you being measured, and which business metrics are most important: margin, safety, productivity, ROE, market share, or turnover?
Organizational Structure
How's your reporting structure? Are decision rights clear and efficient? What about implicit spheres of influence?
Processes
Is it concern about the supply chain that's keeping you up at night? Accounting? Sales fulfillment? Promotion and succession?
External Conditions
From the customers to competitors, regulatory climate to global warming, from local markets to geopolitics.
Assets
Is it intellectual property and branding you worry about, or are you a plant-and-inventory person?
Human Dynamics
Culture, morale, communication, information flow. Any of these can be a hot button.
Metrics
Organizational Structure
External Conditions
Human Dynamics
Assets
Processes

Fig. 7.

After looking at these six categories, Andy added two more items to his initial list:

- "Human Dynamics" had prompted him to think about the change in his relationship with the CEO. There were different structural tensions, different confi-

dences, different expectations. The change had caught him off guard. Andy realized that he needed to think deeply about every aspect of this relationship.
- "External Conditions" had prompted him to look more closely at the realities of his market. Andy realized that his plate was so full that he relied wholly on his team information for perspective on competition and clients. He did not have his own view of this critical aspect of business performance, and that was going to have to change.

After Andy revised his list, it contained nine critical business issues to use as the baseline for his Star of Complexity Map:

- Strategic positioning.
- Revenue: pipeline, backlog, and client relationships.
- New sources of revenue: new offerings, IP rationalization, innovation.
- Talent. (It's critical to the business, and managing "creatives" is different.)
- Profitability/cost structure.
- Changing corporate investment/metrics.
- Synergy with other business units.
- Changing relationship with his CEO.
- Competition and customers.

The next step was to place each of these issues on a vector in Andy's Star of Complexity Map. To assess where he stood with regard to these issues, Andy then needed to look at a set of inherent characteristics that make up the index of his baseline star, as shown in Figure 8.

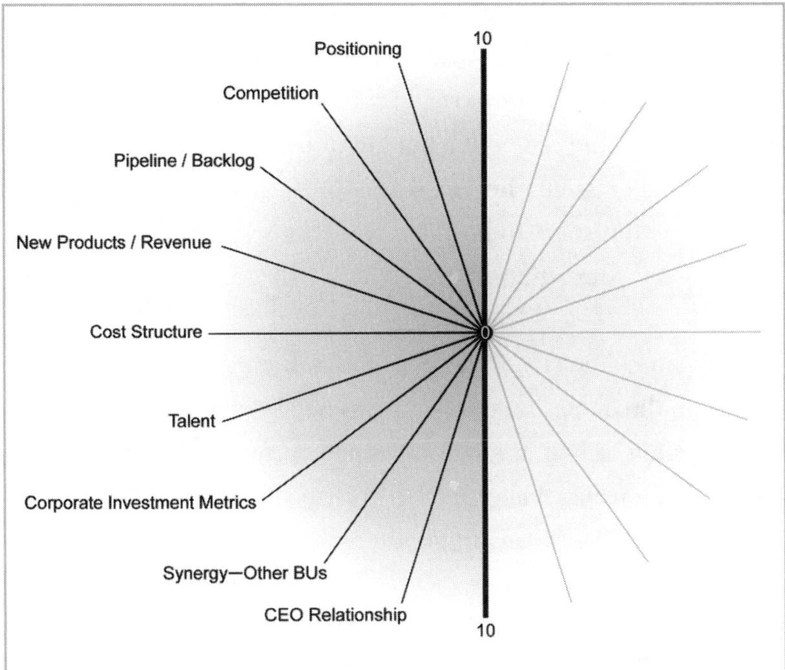

Fig. 8. Andy's Star of Complexity Map shows the nine business issues that are of the greatest importance to him.

Time frame: The time horizon for the challenges he was working on was three years.

Span: The challenges he faced spread across the nine issues he listed.

Interdependence: Virtually any move he planned to make in six of these issues had immediate reverberations on the others, so his overall interdependence index was very high.

Stability: Andy thought his baseline star was fairly stable; that is, he felt that key issues in the star would likely remain relevant for some time.

Criticality: While inaction was not an option, there were no issues where small margins of error were likely to have disastrous or tragic outcomes.

Rate of change: The fluctuation of conditions within the major issues he faced was fairly high, particularly with respect to business conditions, revenue, talent, and competition.

Andy's baseline star, then, looked like Figure 9. When Andy reflected on the index as a whole, it was the "Interdependence" index that leapt out at him and that eventually provided him with a new perspective on his challenge. He realized that he had structured some of his action teams to go after different problems in such a

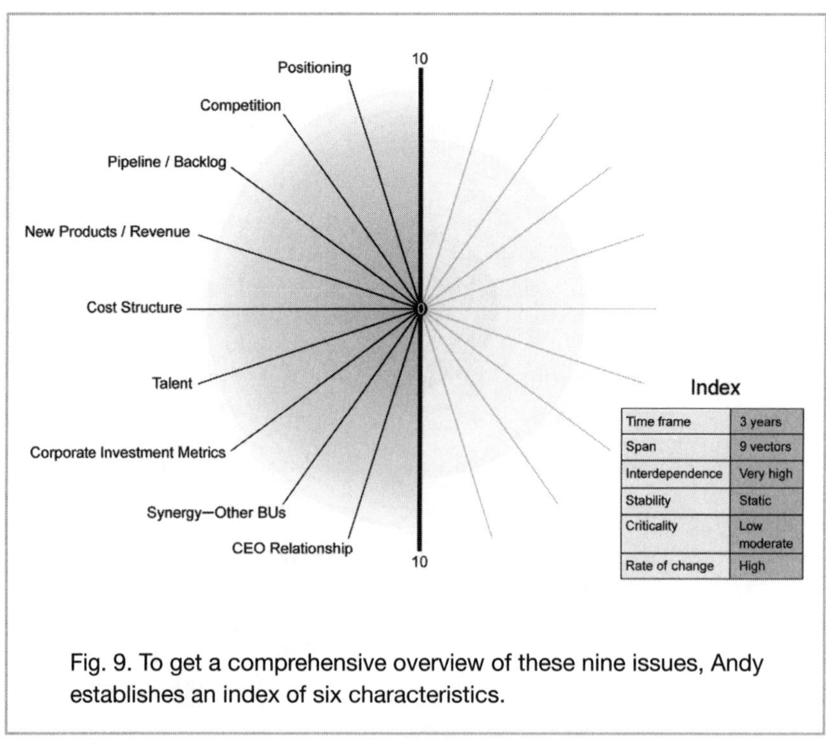

Fig. 9. To get a comprehensive overview of these nine issues, Andy establishes an index of six characteristics.

way that they were likely to come back with good local solutions that still might not work for the entire business.

The next step for Andy was to look at this baseline map through several lenses. By sharpening his focus on different aspects of the star in aggregate, these lenses gave him a useful view of the issues in relation to his resources and to his present knowledge.

I asked Andy to develop a map to illustrate what he saw through each of the three lenses: one map for himself, one for his internal team, and one for his external network.

> Lens 1: self (expertise, exponential thinking, time, and emotional energy).
>
> Lens 2: internal team (expertise, exponential thinking, and structural trust).

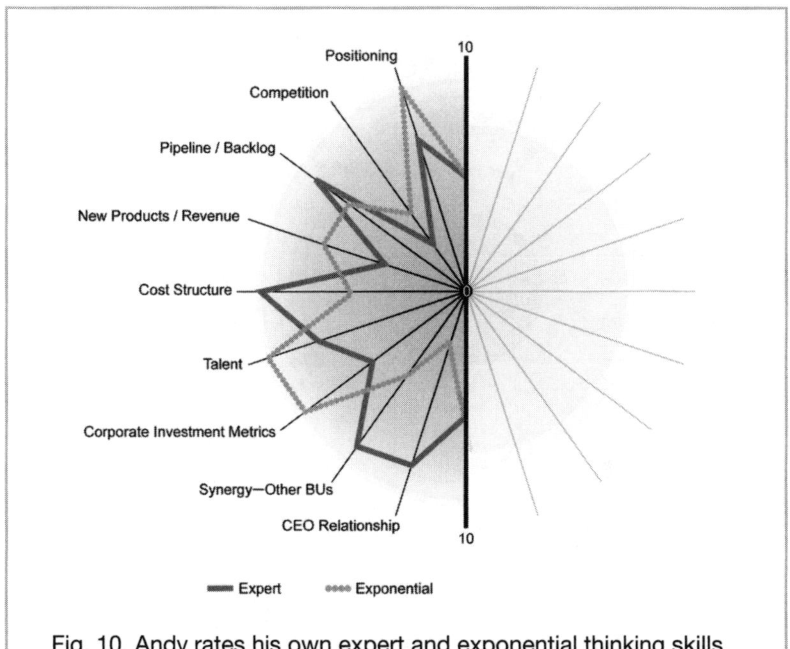

Fig. 10. Andy rates his own expert and exponential thinking skills on each of the nine issues on a scale of 0 (low) to 10 (high).

Lens 3: external network (expertise, exponential thinking, and structural trust).

In the first lens I asked Andy to think about how he applied his own expert and exponential thinking across the issues, using a scale of 0 to 10 (with 0 representing very low expertise, and 10 representing the highest expertise). Figure 10 (page 85) shows what Andy mapped.

The next step was to fill in the right-hand side of the lens with the issues listed in reverse order and apply two more measures: the actual time he spent on each issue and the amount of emotional energy expended on each issue. This is shown in Figure 11.

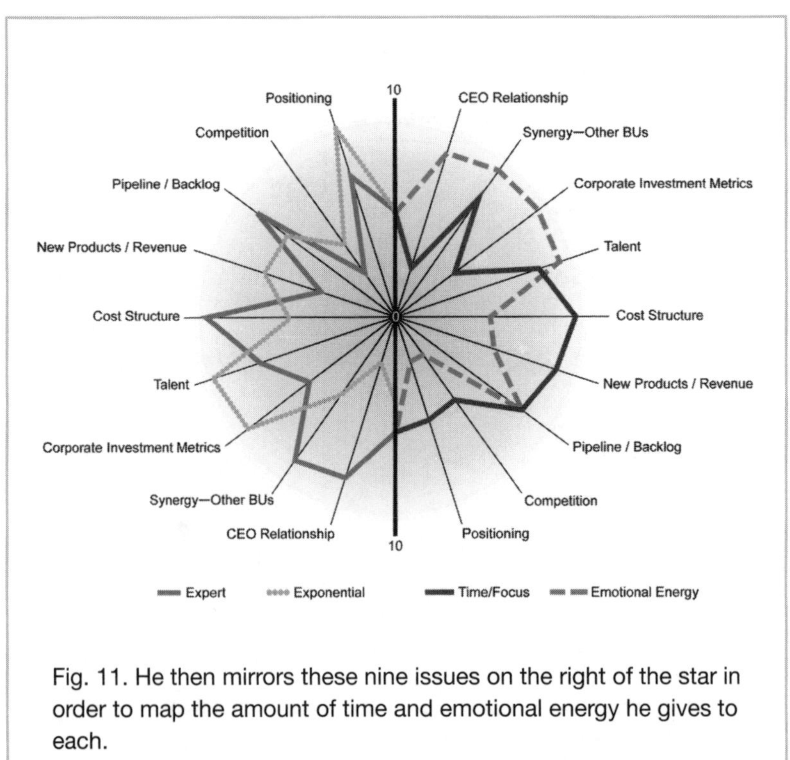

Fig. 11. He then mirrors these nine issues on the right of the star in order to map the amount of time and emotional energy he gives to each.

Looking at his issue of business synergy across both sides of Andy's first lens, he now could see, for example, that he felt he had high expertise but low exponential thinking relative to creating cross-unit synergies. He had a lot of emotional energy about getting this done, because he knew this was key to long-term success, but he was spending only perfunctory time on it, largely because he was not really sure how to make it happen. And his instinct told him that missteps could be very costly.

For the second lens he mapped the same left-hand side issues with regard to his team (Figure 12).

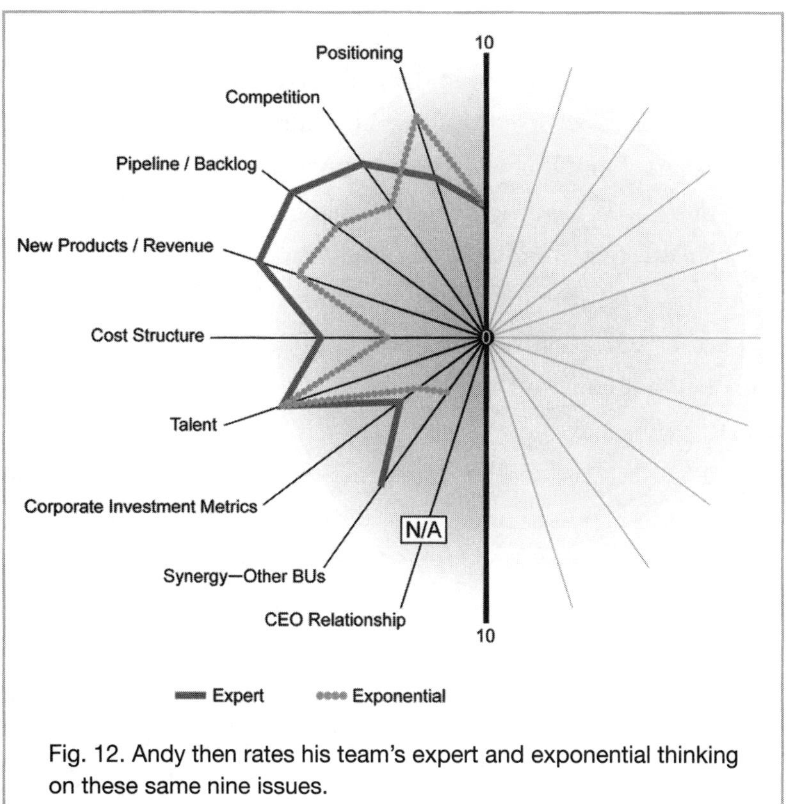

Fig. 12. Andy then rates his team's expert and exponential thinking on these same nine issues.

Andy found it fairly easy to map this part of his team lens. Then I asked him to fill in the right side to reflect his sense of structural trust between himself and his team members on each baseline issue. The purpose of mapping structural trust is to reflect on the question of with whom, and on what topics, you are able to have full disclosure and confidential conversations, and where there are limits and constraints.

When Andy first started to think about the trust side of this lens, he didn't quite see the point of it. This is typical of the key leader stage. His colleagues were brilliant, highly regarded individuals, with many great personal attributes and very high ethical standards.

If there was someone in his organization he could not implicitly trust, he was sure that person would be asked to leave. I encouraged Andy to think about this from the perspective of filters and spin.

"Well, yes, of course I listen with filters and look for spin and self-interest. I'm the new corporate guy here. The stakes are high. Everyone knows that there is inevitable restructuring coming. We may spin off some product lines, integrate others within other parts of the firm. This certainly impacts trust and disclosure."

Further reflection revealed one more important insight: since Andy had not come up through the ranks of the creative staff, he didn't really speak their language, which affected how his people trusted and listened to him. He wasn't yet fluent in what were the most important questions and considerations in their creative work, and he hadn't yet developed the critical perspectives that he was going to need if the acquisition was going to be successful in the long run.

Andy decided to take his time to think about this lens. With these distinctions in mind, he noted his initial thoughts and paid more attention to the issues of spin and advocacy in the next several days.

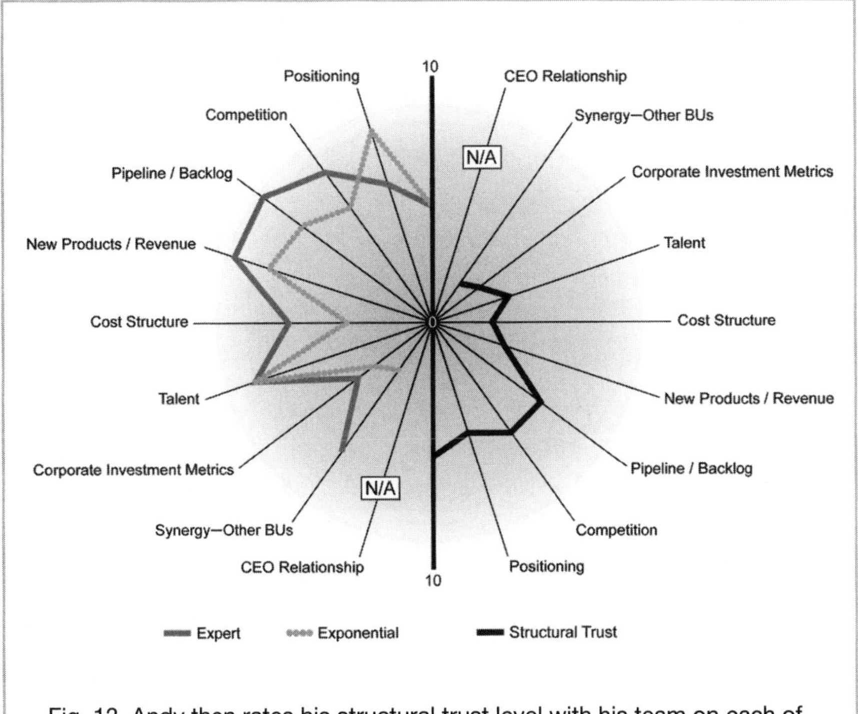

Fig. 13. Andy then rates his structural trust level with his team on each of the issues.

A week later, Andy completed his second map, shown in Figure 13. Andy looked again at the issue of business synergy on both sides of this new lens, noting that his team had little to offer in exponential thinking, and only moderate expertise to bring to the table; moreover, structural trust was low. No wonder he felt isolated and was not making any progress.

The next step was for Andy to map his external network. He prided himself on having a strong network and knowing how to incorporate external perspectives. Given that he tended to ask external people to focus on particular issues, I suggested that he map individuals, instead of trying to map his overall sense of this external team. Andy's third lens looked like Figure 14 (page 90).

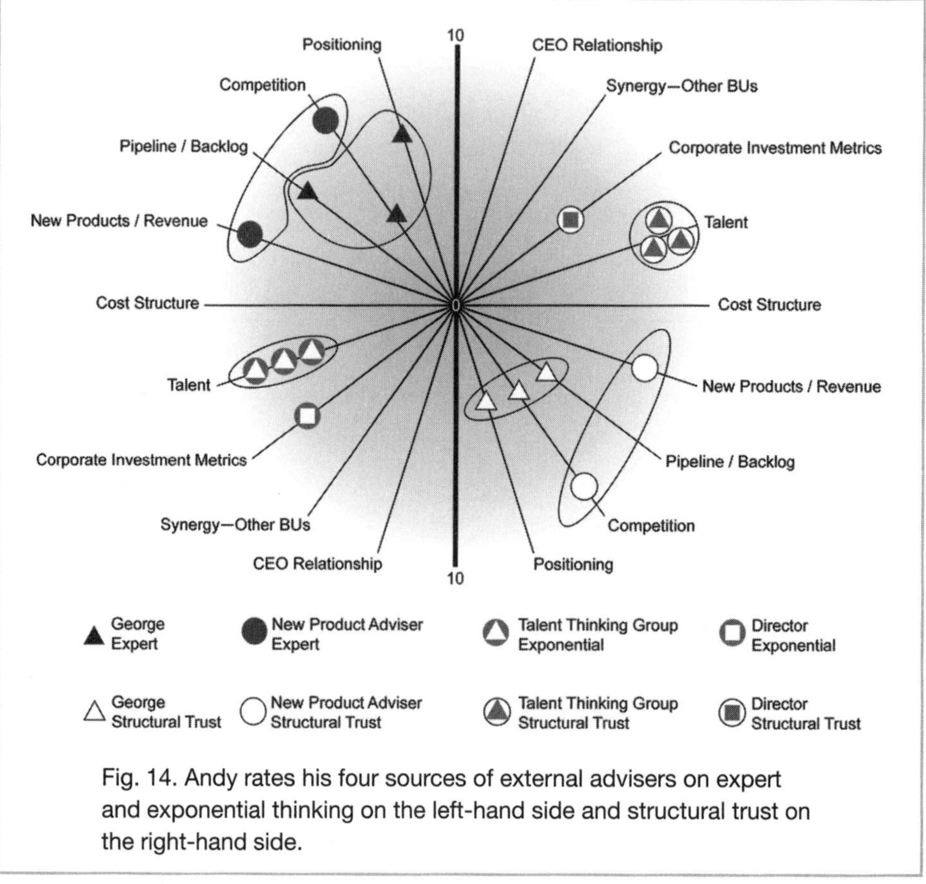

Fig. 14. Andy rates his four sources of external advisers on expert and exponential thinking on the left-hand side and structural trust on the right-hand side.

As Andy thought about his external team, he realized that there were four sets of players, each with different levels of trust and expertise. First, he had inherited a consulting firm that was working on improving positioning and backlog. Andy had spent a fair bit of time with George, the lead partner on this assignment, and found his perspective on many issues helpful. Andy thought of George as an external adviser on positioning, competition, and pipeline/backlog, with low structural trust.

Second, with his VP of new products, Andy found a firm that specialized in new product rationalization. Andy had worked closely with the lead partner, who had extensive expertise in his area, and the joint internal/external team over the past several months. Andy felt this partner also served as an adviser. When he turned to the trust side of this lens, Andy realized that he felt high chemistry with him and no concerns about advocacy and conflict of loyalty.

Third, Andy built his businesses and reputation by being very tuned into hiring and encouraging the best talent he could find. He was a passionate thinker about the nature of talent and how to create organizations so that people can and want to utilize their capabilities to their fullest. Over the years, Andy had found a small group of like-minded executives with whom he often discussed these issues. They would get together from time to time and call each other when they were facing problems. One he met at a conference, another was a key colleague from his former firm, yet another was a research professor on this topic. Over the past few years, he had even started a small "salon"—twice a year he hosted a lunch for people he met who he felt were passionate and knowledgeable about fostering talent.

Andy felt this group had a mix of advisers and thinking partners in it, and he trusted them unequivocally.

Fourth, Andy had a keen interest in economics and how certain measures could be used to drive nonincremental performance. In his former position, he had had the opportunity to work with one of the firm's directors. This director, a well-regarded economist, was working with a small group of corporate staff on reviewing a number of metrics that were in place to drive performance. Andy and this director played golf at the same club, and as they got to know each other, their friendship evolved as well. In his new role, Andy counted on this director as a key thinking partner on the issues of metrics. They continued to have largely informal conversations regarding current economic issues, metrics, and industry outlook. At the same time, they were both aware that there were constraints to the range of their conversation. Andy and this director were careful to keep their conversation at a level that did not draw the director inappropriately into management issues.

The final step for Andy was to bring together key insights to create a whole picture and then to prioritize actions.

I asked Andy to consider both his Star of Complexity Map and the lenses, laying the diagrams side by side, and then to think about three questions:

1. What is most complex and challenging about your role?
2. What is most complex and challenging about your fit within that role?
3. What is most complex and challenging about the way your role is influenced and shaped by others?

(See Appendix I for a more detailed discussion of these questions.)

Andy's work with the maps helped him see the larger, integrated picture of his leadership agenda and teams. First, he realized that he needed to develop deeper appreciation of the expertise around him and of the markets in which he was operating. Yes, he knew a lot about leading professional services businesses, but there were very important nuances in the creative field of his business unit that he needed to understand. He wanted to be able to lead with confidence in unlocking value, and in guiding investment decisions regarding developing new sources of revenue. It was important to him that he develop a deeper understanding of key competitors, trends, and potential industry changes.

Second, he and his team had not thought sufficiently about their underlying business assumptions. What new ways of looking at things might transform their work? They needed a systematic approach to developing new perspectives.

Third, within his operating unit, Andy was more isolated than he imagined he would be. He needed to envision and develop cross-business synergy to create a major success for the overall firm. While he had good relationships with almost every top member of the organization, his new role changed things in ways that he found unfamiliar and sometimes baffling.

Andy concluded that four changes were warranted:

1. He ought to restructure and bring together several independent projects that were highly interdependent. While there were key aspects that could continue as planned, he needed to engage the entire management team in a joint inquiry regarding fundamental assumptions about the business drivers and external environment.
2. He needed to deepen his understanding and perspective on the fundamentals of excellence in the kind of work his staff did, and to better understand and participate in the larger world of this industry. He decided to create a small informal advisory board that would consist of one or two top people in his firm as well as one or two very well known people in the field. He would ask them to structure a series of two-hour meetings that would engage him in developing his perspective, his ability to understand and ask probing questions,

and his general fluency in the content and context of the work. In addition, by networking through this small group, he would participate in events and develop his contacts within this industry.

3. While there were several people inside the firm he thought he could turn to for advice on specific issues, he concluded that he also needed perspective from outside the usual company lenses and dynamics. We agreed that I would continue to be his "big-picture" thinking partner, meeting with him once every quarter to review his overall leadership agenda, mapping all the different issues at stake, and stepping back to look at all the moving parts and interdependencies. I also agreed to spend six months helping him think about how to create greater synergy with the firm: understanding the underlying business issues, cross-boundary and governance challenges, and how his leadership role affected the prospects. We would also focus on whether or not the desire for synergy would lead him to follow the corporate pattern of extending his business unit to all of the firm's major international locations. Finally I would help him offset his isolation as the new guy from Corporate, continuing to support his consideration and development of his in-house and external advisory network.
4. Andy needed a thinking partner to help him understand and sort out the changes he was experiencing in relationship to the CEO. While I could help Andy develop a more sophisticated understanding of some of their interactions, I felt Andy would be best served by someone who knew the CEO and the firm. The senior executive who had originally brought Andy into the firm had retired two years later and was no longer directly associated with the company. Andy

had remained in touch with him and decided to ask for his mentorship in navigating these waters.

Now that we have explored the Star of Complexity Map through Andy's particular case, let's summarize the process:

STAR OF COMPLEXITY MAPPING

Step 1. Start your baseline Star of Complexity Map by writing down your most important issues.

Step 2. Test your initial baseline map for completeness by considering metrics, assets, human dynamics, external conditions, and organizational structure. Add or change as needed.

Step 3. Complete the indices: Time Frame, Span, Interdependence, Stability, Criticality, Rate of Change.

Step 4. Draw the three lenses:

- Lens 1: Leader—Expert/Exponential//Time/Emotional Energy
- Lens 2: Internal Team—Expert/Exponential//Structural Trust
- Lens 3: External Network—Expert/Exponential//Structural Trust

For each lens, what can you see about the strengths and weaknesses of yourself, your team, and your network?

Step 5. With the star, the indices, and the lenses in hand, ask yourself the three Star Mapping of Complexity questions:

What is most complex and challenging about your role?
What is most complex and challenging about your fit within that role?
What is most complex and challenging about the way your role is influenced and shaped by others?

Step 6. Draw conclusions about your focus on exponential inquiry and your time and resources to do so. Assess your current inquiry circles and how you have them deployed. Where do you most need second and third opinions?

Mapping your Star of Complexity is itself an ongoing exercise of leadership inquiry. It guides your Habit of Focus—how you put together your advisory network, develop your inner circle in all four quadrants of your leadership territory, and continue to focus with your inner circle on your non-urgent important work. It requires looking at every aspect of yourself and your environment.

Useful from whenever you begin to develop it, your Star of Complexity Map increases in value as you learn to rely on it over time. It is possible to do this work yourself. However, let me offer this word of caution: other people's perceptions of you and your situation may differ from what you see when you look in your own mirror. It's wise to consider how and when you invite different thinking partners into sounding board conversations about your Star of Complexity Map, exploring different perceptions and contexts that inform it.

CHAPTER 6

The Life Cycle of Your Inner Circle

We have sketched out the terrain of leadership circles and the third opinion through the stories in Chapters 1 and 2. In Chapters 3, 4, and 5 we delineated the Habits of Mind, Relationship, and Focus that leaders need to succeed in the complex era of twenty-first-century leadership. It now remains to explore in some detail how these inner-circle relationships progress through the stages of leadership: beginning with a first assignment as the head of a unit, to the stage of Key Leader, and finally achieving Senior Leadership at the top of an organization.

As we shall see, both the issues of leadership and the ways in which thinking partnerships develop change profoundly over this life cycle. Thus, how to best establish, nurture, and grow the leadership circle relationships that will be essential to your success is the topic that we take up here. Let's return to a story we began in Chapter 1, a story that illustrates many of the issues you will face.

Remember Jim Corliss? He had achieved a major success in the UK and become head of U.S. operations as a result. His accidental discovery of the power of inner-circle advisers in the UK led him to sorely miss his professional relationship with his thinking partner Derek as he found himself facing a new set of challenges in the U.S.

Without fully realizing it, Jim began to search for a few people whom he could ask for those challenging third opinions and unexpected conversations on the wide range of strategic issues facing him in his new assignment.

Several interesting people had caught his attention. There was Brian Stacey, the senior managing partner of a smaller, independent consulting firm, who was leading a project elsewhere in the company. Brian had previously been an executive in a large pharmaceutical company as well as a senior partner at a prestigious strategy firm. Four years earlier, Brian had taken a different tack, deciding to build his own firm as a high-end, niche player dealing with a focused set of strategic issues. As the two men came in contact in the course of the project, Jim noticed once again that here was someone with whom he shared mental click and personal chemistry. Their talks revealed shared intellectual interests that, over time, expanded into new business areas.

Second, Jim found himself working more and more with his new speechwriter, Chris. Jim was impressed with the way Chris helped him take his business thoughts and key messages and transform them into a story that was a memorable whole. Working with Chris was impacting the way he framed things. More and more, he found himself making sure that his messages added up to more than the sum of the key points. He realized Chris shared this way of thinking with Derek, and Jim began to be interested in what else he could learn from Chris.

And third, Jim noticed a staff member on the strategy team, an up-and-coming star, Amin. Amin had a keen ability to sniff out trends, find the little things that didn't add up, and track them down—in the process, coming up with very interesting alternatives. Amin had a natural feel for numbers as well as a balanced view of himself and his gifts. He loved to get to the bottom of things, but not in a way that needlessly exposed others for his own benefit or recognition.

And then Jim's personal ante was suddenly and dramatically raised. He was hired to become the CEO of a major competitor.

That act pushed Jim to develop his inner-circle thinking team in a more intentional way. In his new role, Jim could see clearly how Brian's background and expertise (which included working with boards), along with the developing quality of their conversations, could add to his leadership as a chief executive. Jim asked Brian if he would be interested in a retainer relationship in which they would become regular thinking partners, focused on strategy (long- and short-term), growth, and industry change.

Thus, Jim sought to move Brian from his external-inquiry working circle to his external-inquiry inner circle.

Jim was aware that it was unusual for top partners in firms to take on this kind of unleveraged assignment, because to do it well, without self-interest or advocacy, Brian would essentially be precluded from working to maximize billable work for his own firm. Addressing this problem up-front, Jim suggested that he commit to having his firm hire Brian's firm for a specified amount of work over the next three years. In so doing, Jim wanted to enhance structural trust by removing the need for Brian to sell, and he wanted Brian to meet a reasonable baseline of obligation to his own firm. Someone else from Brian's firm took over the ongoing project work, and Brian focused on his inquiry with Jim.

While this was not a highly leveraged opportunity for Brian, he wanted to become part of Jim's leadership circle. He was interested in the issues at hand, he felt the assignment would be a good use of his expert and exponential thinking, and he liked working with Jim. Their personal trust and chemistry was strong.

Brian took it as a very good sign that Jim and he both understood what it took to create the conditions of high structural trust—and that they were both committed to doing so. For Brian, having the flexibility to pursue this kind of unleveraged work was one reason why he was part of the smaller firm. He had the freedom to make these kinds of business trade-offs.

Over the next few months, Jim let Brian into his inner circle of inquiry. It worked. Brian became a completely confidential sounding board, sparring partner, and external visionary, unencumbered by anything other than a commitment to Jim's success.

In his new role as CEO, Jim needed Chris more than ever. He thought about asking Chris to head up his whole communications group—but when he broached the discussion with Chris, it didn't fly. Chris was flattered, honored, and even tempted, but he knew that the assignment would fundamentally alter his ability to give Jim honest, unbiased feedback. And that was what Jim really needed. It was what was at the core of their powerful working relationship.

Instead, Chris agreed to commit a significant amount of time each month to Jim. In due course, Jim encouraged Chris and Brian to work jointly with him, which enhanced the power of the work the three of them were doing.

Derek also remained in the picture as an intermittent inner-circle thinking partner. Jim continued to turn to Derek when there were issues of high political sensitivity and when he needed to think out a complex set of interactions. Derek also helped Jim to think about the kind of external network of relationships within local communities and with key civic leaders that Jim needed in his new position. It was something that Jim knew was right, and he never would have taken the time for it if Derek hadn't pushed the issue.

Finally, Jim brought Amin with him, again in a key staff role in strategy. Jim asked Amin to help him develop his broad-based advisory network—looking for interesting thinkers whom Jim and his team might benefit from knowing. He gave Amin free reign to think about new lines of sight and relationships that were worth pursuing, both for Jim and also for other leaders on Jim's team.

In the next four years, Jim led the company to record growth, including a major acquisition, and positioned his firm as one of the leading players in the industry.

When Jim joined the firm, this kind of growth was not mandated—and even perhaps not desired—by its conservative board. Acquisitions were not on the agenda either. But as Jim and Brian looked at the business and at the changes in the industry, it became clear to them that a winning future meant acquire or be acquired. Over time, Brian became a key resource to several board members as they rethought their own assumptions and ideas about the business. Jim was in his element, creating a world-class action team, building a major firm, and supported by his external thinking team.

And then, it was time for Jim to step down. He'd had an exciting and highly successful run as CEO. He'd reached the mandated age limit and had a handpicked successor ready to take over.

When Jim finished his term as CEO, he knew he wanted to continue to work, and he wanted to give something back, by sharing his knowledge and skills with the next generations of leaders.

"If I had better understood the power of having a great inner circle, balanced with the right external advisers and thinking partners," says Jim, "I would have been a better leader and matured to my full capacity sooner. Nurturing talent matters to me, and I would have encouraged my best people to develop their own advisory networks with more attention and care, starting from when they were first identified as high potential."

Coming full circle, when Jim retired, Brian invited him to become a thinking partner for himself, as the leader of his consulting firm. Brian also introduced Jim to others in the Fortune 50 where he thought there would be rapport. A few of these developed into highly productive and satisfying inner-circle relationships.

Jim also began developing a venture fund focused on early-stage biotech companies, creating a leveraged way to work with emerging leaders in small companies.

Meanwhile, back in London, Derek had reached the age where he felt it was time to ease off from the rigors of political consulting. The experience of working with Jim had allowed him to see that the range and applicability of his skills and interests went far beyond political consulting, into areas such as business strategy and large, complex partnership deals.

Derek turned his firm over to the next generation of partners, but instead of retiring, he began serving as a thinking partner for CEOs and other senior executives in a range of industries dealing with multiple governments and complex regulatory issues. Far from fading into the background, Derek's work picked up as he entered into this phase. Today, at the age of seventy-four, Derek has served as an inner-circle thinking partner for CEOs and top executives in more than ten major global firms. His longest assignments have spanned twelve years, and some are still running.

How to Build Your Lifelong Leadership Circles

Jim's and Derek's stories illustrate the full life cycle of outside insight and the power that it has to strengthen leadership at several levels. The stories also raise a few issues about how and when to best create, guide, and nurture your advisory networks and teams.

It should be clear by now that these relationships are very powerful leadership resources, precisely because they are full—and fully developed—relationships. By that I mean that while they can begin fortuitously, their care and feeding is anything but accidental, if you want to make full use of their power.

Most leaders, even young ones, have some form of advisory network. It is usually not thought about in a fully systematic way. It happens by accident or out of basic networking skills, but it doesn't go much beyond having a friend to call when you want to chat, or knowing people with whom you can and do trade favors.

As a developing leader, your action team is one that you have probably inherited. You may have limited scope to change it or to shape it into the kind of force for change you would like. But your advisory network is one that you are fully empowered to create, staff, and use. You should populate it with people you really click with, people of the highest caliber, people whom you are completely committed to working with.

This is a team that must be built around you. Its composition and use will necessarily change as your career progresses. You need to start by understanding what you already have in place, and how that currently serves or fails to serve you. Understanding, furthermore, what makes you powerful in exponential inquiry will allow you to build this team to support your strengths rather than merely plugging up your weaknesses. In sports this is called the all-important ability to "bring the game to you."

How should you begin? In the following chapters, we'll discuss how leadership circles should evolve over a lifelong career. While there are no hard and fast demarcations in the stages of leadership, three broad distinctions are useful: Early Leader, Key Leader, and Senior Leader. In general, level of responsibility for the business is a good way to think about your leadership stage. In smaller businesses or flatter organizations, Key and Senior Leaders routinely face decisions across many functional areas that have direct impact on the business. In larger organizations, the Early Leader is someone who is managing something on the order of twenty to fifty people, with a significant role to play in the organization and real decision authority that impacts results. The Key Leader typically leads a strategic business unit or a division. These leaders typically manage multiple groups and often have P&L or large financial responsibility and metrics. In today's world of less hierarchical, more networked leadership, it is not always easy to know when one has crossed the threshold from Early to Key Leader. Some of the largest global corporations make this distinction when they think about their "top two hundred" (or equivalent) leaders. Finally, at the very top levels of the organization, you have the Senior Leaders.

It's never too early—or too late—to start reaching for the third opinion. But my research has shown that the critical juncture for outside insight and inner-circle thinking partners typically comes as leaders develop their stride at the Key Leader level. The cumulative effect of developing your leadership circles grows over the lifetime of your career. Don't wait until you are facing a crisis to start searching for confidants.

Wherever you find yourself now, each of the three chapters that follow will give you practical guidance on how to establish, maintain, and fine-tune your leadership circles. The sections are intended to be cumulative; steps for leaders at the early stages of a career will also be appropriate for leaders at later stages of development if they have not thought about the particular questions involved.

Start Now

Begin by asking yourself:

- What kind of contacts and network have I built, and how and when do I use them?
- Are there teachers, mentors, friends, and activities that have been particularly important in my development at some stage in my life?
- How do I include my spouse or significant other, family members, and personal friends in my current inner circle?
- When have I had a conversation or ongoing dialogue where I significantly changed my understanding or learned something I did not expect? What were the conditions and nature of the relationship that led to the insight?
- Are there critical areas of inquiry for me now where I find I have no thinking partner, or where the thinking partners I have are lacking in expertise, perspective, or appropriate structural trust?

With these questions in mind, let's proceed to understand the issues that present themselves at the three stages of leadership we have delineated: Early, Key, and Senior Leaders.

CHAPTER 7

Early Leaders

Most individuals at the Early Leader level are immersed in mastering the basics of their job responsibilities, in understanding the dynamics of their organizations, and in demonstrating the capability to lead groups to deliver business results. Those business results may be defined by a project, focused on a specific program, or bounded by a territory.

As leaders at this stage develop their outside insight resources, they have two primary things to think about. First, they must learn to develop a few key advisory relationships, to begin to get the third opinion regularly. Second, they must lay the groundwork for their long-term leadership circles.

For the few key advisory relationships, the objectives are to seek expertise, to develop your capacity to apply critical thinking to challenging situations, to break through real and perceived mental barriers, and to accelerate your own development from the lessons of others.

The development of your advisory relationships can and should be done in the context of day-to-day work, and, if done well, will change the trajectory of your ongoing performance. It's about taking a big jump in performance and results, not just perspective. It's about making full use of the all-important third opinion.

Let's look at how Early Leaders should approach developing the Three Habits. (See Figure 15.)

HABIT OF MIND FOR EARLY LEADERS

Improving Exponential Thinking

Corporations recognize and reward those who deliver results. Successful performance not only provides material rewards, but also creates new opportunity. The ability to sort through information, form assumptions, test them rigorously, and then communicate an opinion and offer direction are critical leadership skills that are the foundation of expert thinking. Developing them begins early in one's career.

Exponential thinking goes one level beyond. You look for hidden assumptions, attempt to disprove (rather than prove) hypotheses,

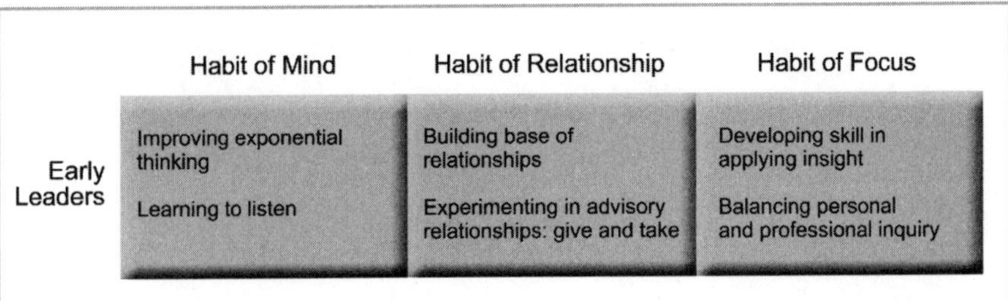

Fig. 15. Early Leaders have the flexibility to experiment as they develop their three habits.

actively seek out the data points that don't fit, and analyze trade-off and risk.

The following exponential questions are the starting point for Early Leaders. Try them, and add your own:

EARLY LEADER QUESTIONS FOR IMPROVING EXPONENTIAL THINKING

- Are there things that I see as clear-cut issues that someone four levels above might see from many perspectives and not as being so clear-cut? Do any of these issues directly affect my excelling at work today?
- Are there issues or challenges that seem persistent or recurrent despite my best efforts to work on them? What are the underlying dynamics that seem to keep me from making progress on these issues?
- Are there things that I know that top management doesn't know that, if they did, would lead them to make very different decisions? What prevents them from knowing these things? What's useful and not useful about their not knowing?
- Are there people I'm working with whose behaviors just don't make sense to me? Is there something about how they see the world that might be very different from my own background and understanding?
- How much flexibility do I have to structure my time? Do I use my time as effectively as possible? How long is the time horizon I'm working on?
- Have there been things that have happened that were

totally unexpected? What do I now do differently to not be caught unaware?
- Are there people who think about things and frame questions in ways that are better than I can, and whom I admire? What makes them able to do that?

These skills are difficult to develop alone. Even if you read extensively and keep up on new theory in a variety of fields, alone, you only hear your own voice trying to sort though all the issues. You'd be well served to find a thinking partner for your exponential thinking. Whether that person is inside or outside your organization, holding your own against a strong opponent is a time-honored way of training the mind.

Learning to Listen

Listening is critical to leadership, and this is an aspect of your work where perception as well as fact matters.

Early Leaders are often chastised for being headstrong and insensitive to the voice of experience. For their part, young leaders often think, I have a fresh perspective, and the organization needs to listen to my modern view of the situation. Both perspectives usually have some merit; however, it is never too early for a leader to develop the ability to listen and learn from others. In this case, it is useful to ask yourself, What are the underlying assumptions of long-timers who see this issue in a traditional manner? What do I see that they don't? Why is that? What do they see or know that I might not? What is an effective way to listen and ask questions that might create a more useful interchange of ideas?

These questions help you integrate multiple perspectives and can also transform your frustration in the face of the old guard, further developing your skills and knowledge. Both of these—greater integration, and greater patience in listening to what seems old-fashioned—will help you as you build your network.

Being conscious of when you are working on inquiry vs. action can also help develop your listening.

Frame your inquiry intentionally; create opportunities to remind yourself to listen—for what's unexpected, what's different, and what's unspoken. When the goal is not to find an answer as soon as possible, you create opportunities to draw out others, to show up in a way that encourages them to participate fully.

Find out what others think of you. It's important to get this feedback, and the earlier you develop this habit the better. There is almost always a significant gap between your perception of your own leadership and that of others around you.

HABIT OF RELATIONSHIP FOR EARLY LEADERS

Building a Base of Relationships

Early Leaders have the potential to cultivate a wide network of contacts both inside and outside the organization. They meet a great many people, but often don't make the most of the opportunity. For some, building a database of contacts is a natural gift, but many others are not completely comfortable building a network that requires asking people to trade favors. Broadening the spectrum of networks to include thinking and sharing perspective has been key for helping some Early Leaders to improve their networking.

EARLY LEADER QUESTIONS FOR BUILDING YOUR BASE OF RELATIONSHIPS

- In addition to the day-to-day interactions, are there people you are more interested in knowing over time?
- Are there things you would do differently if you thought these people would be in your leadership circle for the long haul?
- What happens when some of these people are no longer in your day-to-day world?
- How effective are you at cultivating and maintaining relevant contact with people when you are not in active contact on daily issues?

As we noted earlier, the finer distinctions of structural trust that shape the boundaries of inner- vs. working-circle relationships are often not as relevant for the Early Leader. But noticing whom you would want to work with over time is highly relevant, and worth beginning to cultivate early. Are these distinctions based on a sense of chemistry?

On a way of thinking together? On trust? On their current position? On your sense of their career trajectory? What else draws your attention and interest? *It's your network.* What's important, and what works, for you?

This is also the time to begin to experiment with breadth—how broad a base of people can you engage in ways that are relevant to your challenges and results?

Here are some approaches to developing a broad-based network:

- Increase the probability of accidental relationships emerging. Volunteer for task forces, participate in industry trade groups, and assist on special projects. Also, don't forget to ask. Potential thinking partners may be flattered that you believe their insight and support have value.
- In some cases, there is power in numbers. You can pull together a group of colleagues, classmates, or peers to seek perspective from a key individual more efficiently than you can do it alone. Offer to take him or her to breakfast; offer to create a dialogue.
- In reaching to a senior person, look for opportunities to share perspective from your vantage point. Your view of the world may be valuable to the Senior Leader you are looking to connect with. Senior people have a real sense of legacy. They are often looking for bright young people to help. Senior people like to be associated with winners in the next generation. Keep track of them as you move forward and find appropriate ways to support them or acknowledge their contributions to your success. Be judicious and appropriate about managing requests for time.
- Let relationships evolve over time. Begin by asking for input on an issue. Be thoughtful about questions that help you sense your mental click with the other person and theirs with you. Be specific with your questions and open to the answers. Ask for the opportunity to come back.

Because you are looking for a wide range of application, expert, and exponential thinking, many individuals can contribute to your advisory network. To take the mystery out of how you can begin to develop contacts, here is a brief discussion of where your network members are mostly likely to be found.

Corporate Contacts

Don't underestimate even the most passing contacts within your own organization. An advisory network for an Early Leader includes people beyond her specific organizational unit and may include a wide range of individuals within the corporation. Executives who interviewed you during the hiring process, leaders who participate as development coaches and mentors, and leaders with specific expertise or talent can all be useful resources.

Academics

Business school professors, graduate school contacts, and faculty advisers are often happy to continue in a thought partner relationship with former students. Interestingly, even faculty with whom you may not have had a close relationship during school, if contacted about an issue or market they are following, often are eager to partner with leaders in exchange for a direct observation of their theories or a market at work.

Trade Associations/Trade Shows

Large gatherings and institutional collections of individuals who work in a specific industry or topic area can be an excellent source of expert and application thinking. Gaps in expert thinking during the early career are often the result of a limited time in an industry, and these organizations can provide a useful foundation of specific information about a given market or technology. At all stages of leadership, expert thinking in a public forum can provide valuable external thinking for an executive. Over time, customization of the content to your specific issues becomes more critical, but at the Early Leader stage any perspective that lifts you up from your day-to-day focus can provide vital perspective on your challenges. Using industry seminars to expand your perspective, and building skills and contacts through training programs and seminars can be useful as well.

Partners/Alliances

Increasingly, Early Leaders are the key day-to-day contact points working across boundaries: functional, organizational, alliance, and external. While this can be frustrating, it has the potential to be immensely valuable. Be intentional in creating alliances and look for instructive differences. It can be incredibly useful to work closely with someone who isn't shaped by the same organizational culture and bias. While recognizing that discretion is critical in any arm's-length relationship, you may find potential thinking partners and advisers within a partner organization more readily than within your own.

Job Search Contacts

One benefit of a job search (particularly if it represents a career change) is that it can be an invaluable source of potential contacts, who can become future advisers, once you begin to shape your role in an organization.

Alumni Networks

Most undergraduate and graduate schools have local alumni organizations. Active participation in these events, and in the organization and leadership of these activities, can help make contacts with executives in other organizations with years of relevant experience. Those contacts can be relatively easy to make with the common school thread in your background and can provide a fertile ground of potential advisers on a wide variety of topics.

Nonprofit Activities and Nonwork Organizations

These activities aren't only rewarding emotionally; they can also provide you with access to individuals who may be useful thinking partners, but would be inaccessible to you through other channels.

Identify multiple resources to provide perspective in your advisory network. Some will be anxious and eager to assist you; others may be unwilling or simply not have the time. Having a backup plan is useful. Don't be concerned if you don't connect with every individual you contact. And remember, an advisory relationship needs to be a good fit both ways to be valuable. It's up to you to shape these relationships with value creation for both parties in mind.

Experimenting with Different Kinds of Advisory Relationships, both Receiving and Giving as a Thinking Partner

At this stage, you are building a set of skills to use outside thinking well. This is the best time to experiment. Try to identify a range of people with different types of thinking to offer and different personal styles. The relative risk of advice and counsel from others is low. This point is worth thinking about. The more senior you become, the bigger the risks you will have to manage. You need advice and outside insight, but it can be risky. Everyone has had the experience of taking the advice of a friend and having things work out badly. It's at this stage of your leadership that you can best afford to try a range of experiments and hone the skills that work for you.

Seek out a thinking partner relationship with a few people on specific issues. Keep it focused on your essential non-urgent agenda, as we've discussed in previous chapters. Be careful about advice, that is, the "here's what I think you should do" conversation. Rather, see how you can engage in conversations that broaden perspective and options, and that help you see yourself and your choices more clearly.

Not only do you need to identify whom to contact, but you need to consider how to work with them as well. You need to explore what approach to thinking partners will work for you. Someone to engage in active dialogue? Someone to provide you with rich perspective that you can reflect on privately? Someone to challenge your initial assumptions about your role? Someone who will help you consider the broader implications?

Experiment with doing some reciprocal thinking-partner work in a small group. Notice what's powerful and limiting about this. Can you use a group setting to test your ideas or do you need more private interaction?

Recognize that as thinking-partner relationships become more individual, there is a significant element of chemistry that shapes an effective dynamic. What may work well with one individual may not work well with another. Being familiar with multiple styles of interactions is an asset as you build and enhance your leadership circles in the future.

Begin to pay attention to how you calibrate and filter the insights and opinions of others. Knowing how to judge people and their contributions, and knowing how to form and test your independent judgments, takes time.

Look to give as a thinking partner to someone else. What do you learn about what it takes to be a good thinking partner vs. telling someone your opinion? What motivates you to persist in thinking with and supporting someone else's exponential thinking? What does this teach you about what you are looking for in potential thinking partners? What does this teach you about how to be someone who attracts great thinking partners to work with you?

HABIT OF FOCUS FOR EARLY LEADERS

Developing the Skill to Apply Insight That Drives Results

One critical objective at the beginning of building and using your advisory network is learning how to get results from insight. New ideas and insight come from all three kinds of thinking: application, expert, and exponential. For example, application thinking with external data might help you get insights into calibrating time frames for projects, or discovering a key resource needed for a special activity. External expert thinking can be used to create ways to think about sizing a newly defined market segment or finding a highly specialized potential business partner. Exponential thinking might drive you to identify a whole new market for an existing product. Knowing what to do with what you learn is the difference between an academic exercise and truly powering up your leadership capacity.

Armed with a new insight, what's next? How do you go about putting this understanding to work?

How to proceed is not always straightforward. Early Leaders do well to be thoughtful about why an idea is new. Why has no one thought of it before? Does it have a history? Why do you think it will work now? Then you need to think carefully about stakeholders. What is effective in getting others to embrace the idea and be willing to do something with it? Developing skill and instinct in stakeholder mapping is a key part of moving insight to results.

EARLY LEADER QUESTIONS FOR GETTING RESULTS FROM INSIGHT

- Is there a pattern in how you go about trying to use new insight?
- How well do you understand the full range of stakeholders for your new idea?
- How often do you see a new idea through to a result? How often do such ideas slide onto the list you never get to?
- How do you calibrate which ideas are most likely to have big impact?
- How easy is it for you to get sidetracked?

Keep focused on the important non-urgent issues. Use a tool like the Star of Complexity to map the crucial non-urgent issues and track your time, energy, and focus on these. Working with a special adviser on how to focus insight for results is often a good point of concentration for an early-stage advisory relationship. Having a thinking partner with whom you track and discuss the ways in which you attempt to use insight is very helpful in moving beyond being someone with lots of good ideas to someone who uses innovative ideas to get good results—which is often the biggest factor in how fast you move from Early Leader to Key Leader.

Balancing Personal and Professional Inquiry

At this stage, many individuals continue to agonize over their career choices, second-guessing the fit between their current path and their interests and talents. As they seek outside guidance, they often confuse getting personal coaching with using a thinking partner and developing their range in the three Habits.

While one vector of your Star of Complexity Map may relate to career considerations, these issues should not be allowed to overwhelm your approach to inquiry. You need balance, and the use of your thinking partners needs to be weighted toward the business and leadership issues you face.

How Early Leaders Establish Their Networks

It's time to get practical and to see how outside insight plays out in real situations. Let's look at several examples of Early Leaders and their early leadership circles.

An honors graduate of Georgia Tech, Elizabeth Kelly has never had a moment's doubt about her skills as an engineer. But now, three years into her career with a major oil-and-gas company, she is feeling less confident about other aspects of her performance.

Nine months ago, Elizabeth was promoted to lead a project that's a small (fifteen to twenty people) but important part of a larger infrastructure construction project. The project was expected to take two to three years and required coordination with a range of other initiatives as well as construction programs at key suppliers. In addition, several of the critical technologies that her team planned to use were still in prototype and would need to be continually evaluated for feasibility throughout the project.

As she dealt with multiple stakeholders and sorted through the many roles and responsibilities that remained unclear, she became concerned, not just about her individual performance, but about the overall success of the project. She was working long hours, get-

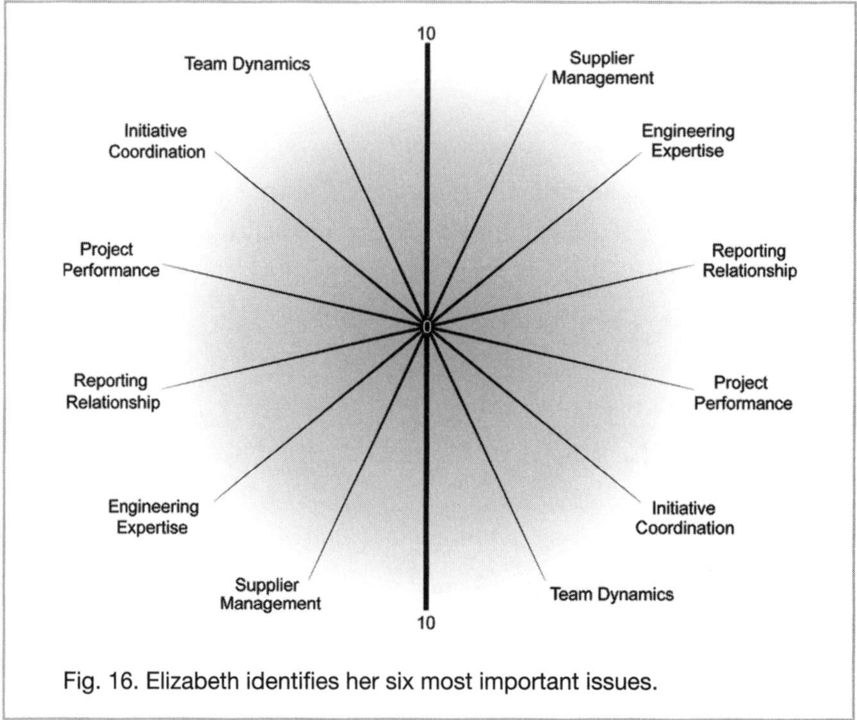

Fig. 16. Elizabeth identifies her six most important issues.

ting good feedback and encouragement from the people around her, and yet she wasn't sure that things were going to come together. People really seemed to trust her leadership and her can-do attitude. So why did she always have that sense of missing something? What was it about this project that made her feel so unsure at the end of each week that real progress had been made? Elizabeth needed a third opinion.

When I connected with Elizabeth, I suggested that she use the Star of Complexity Mapping tool as a way to look at her overall leadership. What she really wanted was to have more confidence in her ability to guide her team to deliver the overall result they were after.

First Elizabeth mapped her baseline as in Figure 16. Elizabeth's

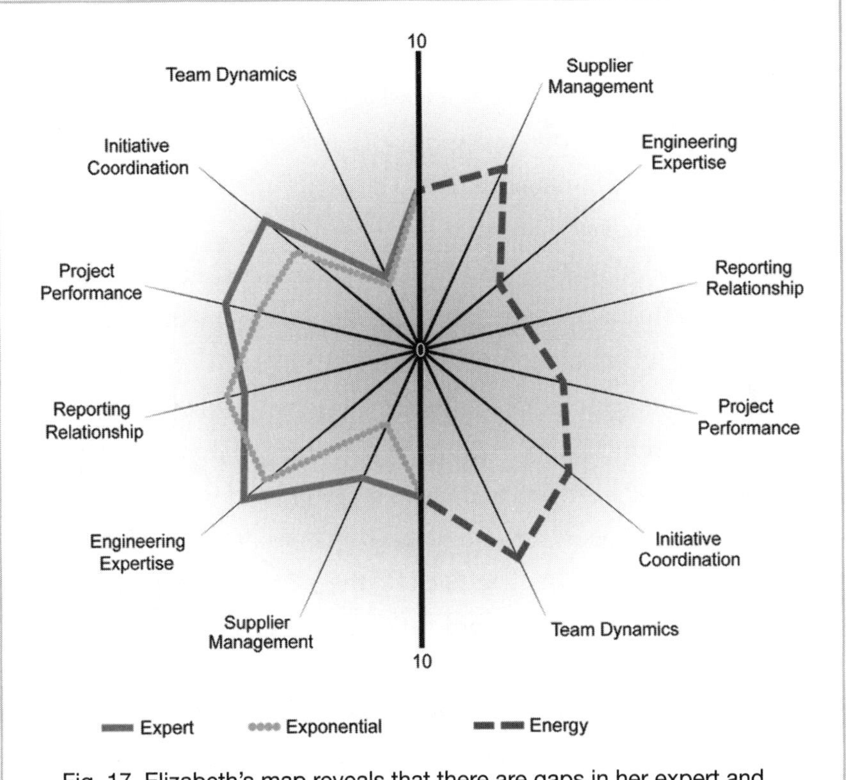

Fig. 17. Elizabeth's map reveals that there are gaps in her expert and exponential thinking as well as that she is spending more and more time on areas of her least expertise.

baseline was appropriately focused on her project and bounded by the issues that she faced on a day-to-day basis.

Elizabeth then mapped her star's complexity as she looked at her relative strengths of expertise and exponential thinking, as well as how she was spending her time and energy. (See Figure 17.)

Elizabeth's map revealed the strength she felt in her technical performance, and her sense of her ability to lead the team in assessing the needed emerging technologies. It also showed her self-perceived gaps in both expert and exponential thinking in how to handle the issues of team, supplier management, and initiative coordination. Further, it showed that she was spending more and more of her time on her areas of least expertise and confidence. Was that part of the new role that came with her promotion, or a sign of her being on new ground, or both?

Her map suggested several things to Elizabeth. First, she saw that she needed to significantly develop her expertise and knowledge about team dynamics and supplier management. Next, she needed to find people to have thoughtful and safe dialogues about the interdependencies of the issues she faced. How will the new technologies function? What are the potential pitfalls for a complex project like this one? Are there ways to go beyond the normal tools for project management and initiative coordination that will be more effective? Can she cut back on the ever-escalating time that seems to be required for coordination and get back to the real science? Finally, how does she continue to see her team's work inside the overall goals and commitments of her division?

For the first time, Elizabeth has begun to think exponentially about her role. As such, she will be developing her abilities to think in this new way, and she will be learning to listen. She had been doing what most people do in unfamiliar, stressful situations: applying her usual thinking patterns to new conditions. But because she didn't know how to listen for what was really being talked about, she didn't hear the issues with team dynamics that were being aired. She also dismissed and cut short informal conversations with key suppliers who would drop by her office to chat when, in fact, they were attempting to get some vital information to her ahead of their formal contractual reporting mechanisms. Thus, she had been unable to gather key information, identify certain issues, and resolve these problems. Equipped as she was with a strong engineering background, she was far more comfortable solving technological issues than people and perception issues. She had been spending more and more time on areas where she was less and less comfortable, a familiar problem for new Early Leaders.

As a new Early Leader, Elizabeth needs to make progress on all of the three Habits for Early Leaders presented at the beginning of this chapter, but most especially the first Habit's two elements: thinking and listening. As she begins to develop her Habit of Mind, this will guide her early Habit of Relationship, where she will start to establish the networks, relationships, and apprenticeships that can power up the kinds of help she needs and the education she requires. With that, the skill and balance will eventually come.

Let's look at another case.

Kurt had been an internal consultant for a major Fortune 50 company since graduating from business school. For seven years he had successfully run and implemented strategy and restructuring projects in several business units, and had most recently been responsible for developing the business specifications for an enterprise management software application that was successfully installed across the four largest divisions of the company. Aware that he still lacked substantial line responsibility, he jumped at the opportunity to take on the Service Division of the Medical Products Group. When he arrived, however, he was rapidly overwhelmed. Customer issues arose quickly and had to be resolved immediately. Much of Kurt's skill at managing large-scale projects was irrelevant. He had to improve service levels dramatically, but he had to do it while continuing to deliver service. In addition to this challenge, his management team, although friendly, was skeptical that an internal consultant could lead their group. It was time for a third opinion.

Kurt's Star of Complexity looked like Figure 18 (page 126). The eight vectors reflected the complex dynamics facing him and his organization. He had strong exponential thinking available to him in

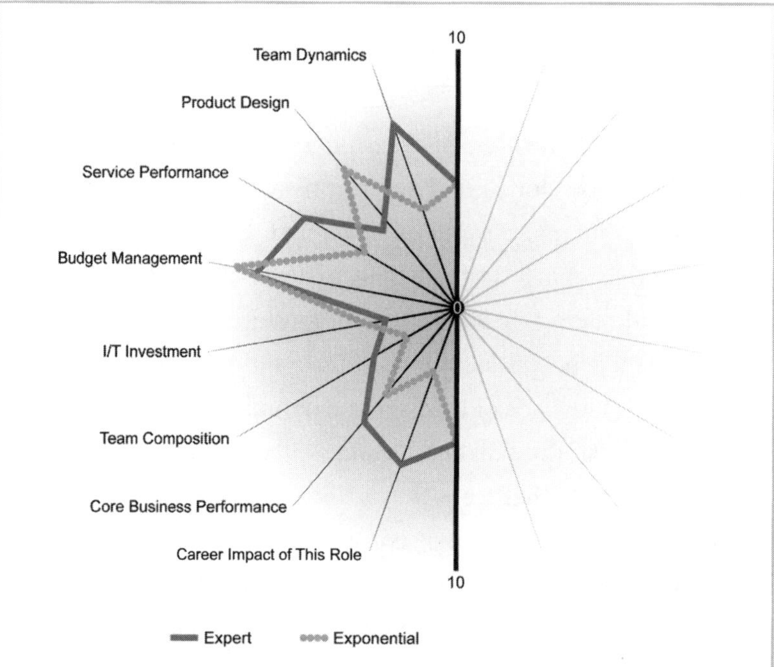

Fig. 18. Kurt's Star of Complexity Map shows that not only does his expertise need strengthening in certain areas, but he also needs advisory resources to help him think outside the box.

several areas, but realized that he was very low on advisory resources, and on his own ability to think through the interdependency of the service performance issues. He faced major choices about upgrading systems, redesigning processes, and changing the pricing structure for his group's work, and each choice had significant implications for the others.

Kurt's number-two staffer, Allesandro, was committed to the Services Group and, unlike Kurt, expected to make his career there. Allesandro resented Kurt being brought in over him. Considerable friction with key personnel was thus inevitable unless Kurt could find a way to enlist Allesandro's support.

In talking his dilemma over with his spouse, Nicole, Kurt got a suggestion that turned out to be the beginnings of a solution. Nicole told him that rather than seeing Allesandro as an adversary, it would be better to give him more responsibility. That might increase the probability that Allesandro would get the top job when Kurt moved to his next assignment. "Don't you know anyone who knows something about the service industry?" she asked. "Some old business school professor of yours?"

That was the other suggestion he needed to show him a way forward. Kurt called a former business school professor with deep customer service expertise. This new thinking partner brought deep expert thinking in the field and was able to grasp the specific dynamics of his situation. Together they were able to discuss multiple business models for a customer service organization and debate in real depth the pros and cons of each. Kurt found the discussion helped both to frame the issues more clearly and to provide a sequence for the decisions he faced. As soon as Kurt was comfortable, he brought Allesandro into the conversations with his professor. Wary at first, Allesandro discovered he liked the professor. Allesandro quickly developed a better understanding of where Kurt's thinking was headed and now felt that Kurt trusted him because of bringing him in and developing their thinking together.

Kurt began a two-tiered program to improve the current service and to redefine the business for the future. He gave Allesandro leadership of the day-to-day problems while he worked on the restructuring design. He enlisted Allesandro's support by positioning him as both a great operational leader and as having a key role in the longer-term, more strategic changes. Kurt told Allesandro that he viewed him as his successor, and he offered to design Allesandro's role with that goal in mind. He also asked for Allesandro's input in creating this role, as well as that of other key players in the group.

Thus Kurt began to gain valuable experience in applying insights to drive business results, thanks to his early advisory network of spouse and former business school professor.

For a final example of an Early Leader and her network development, let's look at Eleanor, who was also overwhelmed by tough business issues. For six years she managed an industrial software product line for a major software company. The application set that Eleanor was responsible for provides small businesses with regulatory record keeping. While it hadn't happened yet, Eleanor knew that her stand-alone product sales were in jeopardy of declining as customers were starting to expect this functionality as part of broader suites of software products. Eleanor was in a quandary about the best next step for the business. License this product to other suppliers for integration? Shift the application design to continue to represent an alternative to the big providers? Shut down the group? It was time for a third opinion.

In managing the business, Eleanor has followed a highly leveraged model: all marketing has been outsourced to an industrial software advertising and marketing firm, much of the software development was done by contract developers, and the sales force (although internal) sold many products, not just this application. When asked, Eleanor said that she had an incredibly strong team, in part due to this structure. That was why she felt her Star of Complexity was very strong in almost all points on expert and exponential thinking. However, as she began to frame alternatives for the product, Eleanor realized that each member of her virtual leadership team had a strong bias about the available options, shaped by their roles in their own organization as well as their roles on her virtual team. She realized that she needed a thinking partner or partners who could help sort through the options and the far-reaching implications of each from a wider perspective on the business, not just a particular functional vantage point. Figure 19 shows Eleanor's Star of Complexity.

Eleanor turned first to a peer business unit head, with whom she had worked at length in the past, to help think strategically about her options. In addition, she turned to the leader of an industry trade group who she felt knew all the competitors and players in the marketplace. She asked for help in both framing the alternatives and understanding the potential implications of her actions.

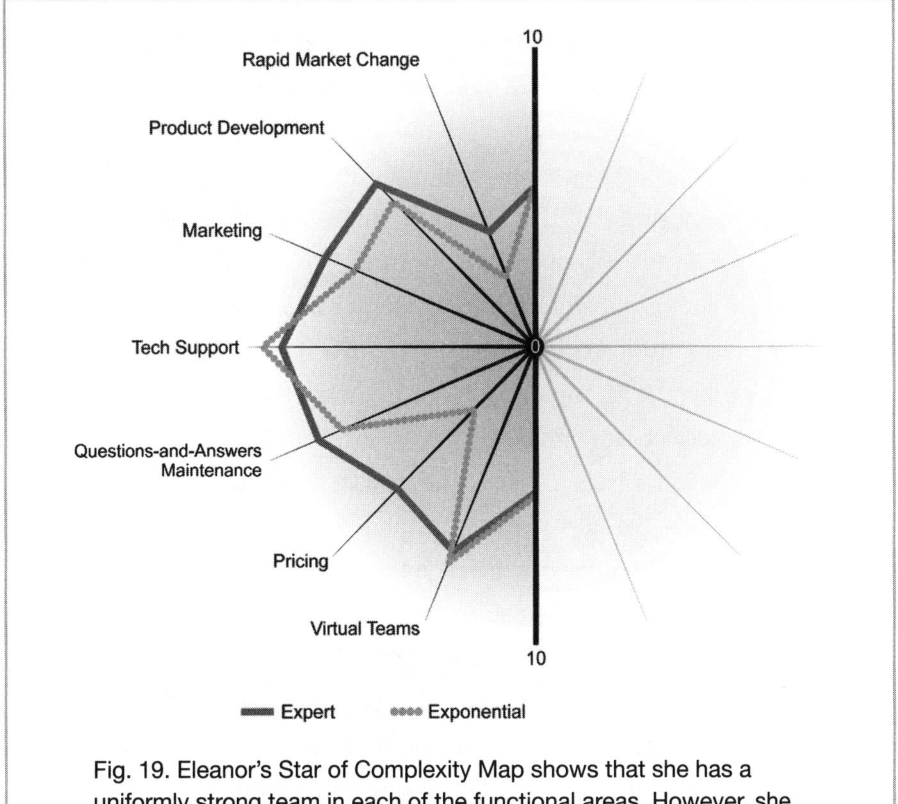

Fig. 19. Eleanor's Star of Complexity Map shows that she has a uniformly strong team in each of the functional areas. However, she realizes she needs a broader perspective on the business.

Eleanor's thinking partners identified a critical gap in her Star of Complexity: she had only limited understanding of the corporate implications of the decisions she faced. What would licensing this application mean for the broader corporate product line? Would she be responsible for channel conflict between her company's products and their competitors? How could she get other business unit leaders on board to support her plan?

With this additional dimension of complexity clearly in mind, the thinking partners began to help Eleanor understand the goals for a transition in the business. They also helped her frame her alternatives. As Eleanor said, "Without their counsel, I would have made several key choices for the wrong reasons. I needed to step back and think about what I was really trying to accomplish, and then what it would take to get there. I was really focused on 'just getting *it* done' without being sure that the *'it'* was the right thing to be doing."

Eleanor eventually managed to "sell" the product to a much larger product group within the company, embedding the software in the more extensive package. Thus, the team was saved and Eleanor moved with the product, first leading the work of embedding her product's functionality into the larger suite. The new group felt they had a lot to learn from Eleanor about designing and managing effective virtual teams. After about six months in her new group, she was promoted to manage the partnerships-and-alliances team for the entire product suite.

Eleanor learned how to think exponentially about the relationship of her product to a rapidly changing market inside a much broader understanding of her overall company and its many disparate divisions. In this way, she learned to be effective with the other internal product leaders and to successfully lead a major change not yet detected as necessary by Corporate. As an Early

Leader, she discovered that her passion for her job and the product would only carry her so far. Beyond that, exponential thinking and a broader base of relationships were key.

AN EARLY LEADER'S HABIT OF FOCUS CHECKLIST

- ✓ Use the Star of Complexity Map to frame and focus your advisory relationships.
- ✓ Identify potential resources and reach out to them.
- ✓ Experiment with the characteristics of advisory relationships that would be most useful to you.
- ✓ Establish a time commitment.
- ✓ Work on using the insights.
- ✓ Set milestones for considering the state of your advisory network and revising or reminding yourself of next steps.
- ✓ Renew the cycle.

Use the Star of Complexity Map to Frame and Focus Your Advisory Relationships

1. Develop your Star of Complexity Map as the baseline to guide your assessment of opportunities and needs. Test your map with peers and others who understand your responsibilities and performance. These perspectives will add useful insights. Revisit the map periodically, especially as you build your own skills. Gaps in expert thinking can be closed quickly at this stage of an individual's career.

2. Evaluate your Star of Complexity Map through the lenses and determine your gaps.

Think broadly about your map—not just about your current task, but about the entire project or business operation. Think about not just your current job but your current trajectory. Think about not just the current challenges but ones you might expect to face at the next stage of a project or job.

3. Prioritize your needs based on your current map.

You need to invest in relationships that provide support for your current work, but also create opportunity to build a platform for the future.

You cannot work on all the issues simultaneously, and one of the critical skills to build at this stage is the discipline to prioritize. Do try to work on gaps in all three kinds of thinking. Building your own skill across all three areas will enable you to differentiate both your needs and your counsel in the future.

Identify Potential Resources and Reach Out to Them

Explicitly identify multiple resources to provide you with the types of insight you believe that you need. Not all will work out. Reach out to each of them with a specific, single objective for the initial contact and then be willing to frame the next steps as a result of the first interaction.

Experiment with the Characteristics of Advisory Relationships That Would Be Most Useful to You

This is the stage of your career to consider *how* you think and make decisions. You need to explore what approach to thinking partners will work for you. Being familiar with multiple styles of interactions is an asset as you build and enhance your leadership circles in the future.

Establish a Time Commitment

Building and developing your inquiry skills and advisory network is not a short-term project, nor is it something that will happen without conscious attention. You need to focus yourself to make it happen.

Work on Using the Insights

You need to be conscious of your cognitive style; for example, do new ideas come to you during discussion or during reflection? You will then need to be disciplined to ensure that you take action based on the insights you have gathered.

Set Milestones for Considering the State of Your Advisory Network and Revising or Reminding Yourself of Next Steps

These are useful to ensure that you are building the relationships and contact network that you need, but also to remind you to get back on track if you have stopped using your advisory resources on a regular basis.

Renew the Cycle

Continue to assess your Star of Complexity Map to ensure that you are building a focus on the important non-urgent issues into your work habit and routine, and that you are tapping into resources that can best help you to deliver on current performance and define future opportunity.

CHAPTER 8

Key Leaders

Francois Cleune worked his way up from the ranks at a Canadian manufacturing company. He had a passion for making things operate well, with high productivity and results. As part of his career development, he was offered the opportunity to take a major leadership position in a new U.S. technologies and troubleshooting group, which was transforming from a cost center to a profit center, with a mandate to serve the company and other external clients.

Francois believed in hard work, skill, and owning the responsibilities of his position. At the same time, he always understood that large, complex organizations and industries are interlocking networks of people, and he was mindful of his network. Early in his career Francois developed his Habit of Relationship, looking for people with line of sight and ideas that stretched his own. He developed relationships with mentors, and mentored many people himself. He instinctively understood the value of the third opinion.

When Francois signed on as president, U.S. and Canada, Strategic Technologies Business Unit, he knew he was in new territory and that he needed some help. He initially sought out a technology visionary who was also working with his boss. This relationship was very productive early in his tenure, and then tapered off, though it remained friendly.

His new position required that Francois step up to a level of work that he had not known before. In addition, he became a member of the board of the U.S. subsidiary, his first board experience, with global players. He knew there were areas where he had little to no experience or background, and that he needed to develop his ability to lead in these areas quickly. Focusing first on issues of global leadership across cultures and countries, Francois added to his advisory network an executive coach, who helped him broaden his perspective on global leadership and improve the effectiveness of his communication style.

About a year later, Francois was wrestling with some complex commercial and organizational issues. The strategies that he had inherited from senior leadership were self-contradictory in certain ways, and as a Key Leader, Francois was not able to change them—at first.

No one on the inside had extensive experience in these issues, so it made sense to Francois to bring in outside perspective and expertise to ensure that the company didn't "drink its own Kool-Aid."

When Francois mentioned this to his technology adviser, Adam, he suggested that this might be a time for Francois to look for a primary thinking partner who had a broad range of experience in the commercial aspects of high tech, large-enterprise clients, and complex global organizations. At first Francois thought he was suggesting that he hire a management consulting firm to do a strategy study, but that was not what Adam had in mind. Instead, Adam suggested that Francois should define a few small inquiry projects so that he could try working with several different types of senior external resources as he developed his thinking and expertise in these new areas.

I was asked to undertake one of these projects; from our first meeting we both felt that "mental click" and quickly began developing a sense of shared trust. Francois saw that I could offer a brand new line of sight, lots of experience, and mental models, but also that our dialogue would help him cut through the complexity and enable him to try on different lenses that would clarify the global nature of some of his problems.

I didn't do the thinking for Francois, but my fresh perspective helped enhance his leadership. In addition, he learned early that he could count on me for expertise and the unvarnished truth. In one instance, a conversation about new market competition and industry changes led me to challenge Francois to take a second look at the underlying assumptions that had guided funding of several major internal projects that Francois had inherited. As we continued to think about these changes, Francois realized that there was one project in particular that he needed to look into. Within a few weeks, he had saved something on the order of $100 million by asking the project team a new set of questions that enabled him to conclude that the project should be canceled before it caused the company both harm and financial loss.

All companies find some way to bring outsiders in—but each company culture has different levels of openness and ways of working with outside experts. In this case, outside help was fine as long as it was related to an expertise the company didn't itself possess. Francois brought several of us onto his inquiry team and made the presence of the outsiders known to his action team. Over time, a few of these relationships evolved into inner-circle thinking partnerships.

Francois was clear with his internal teams that the technology adviser, executive coach, and I were part of his leadership team. At times we attended meetings with him—other times without him.

He encouraged me to get to know some of his key people and to help develop their thinking about business models and the high-tech services world much as I had done with him. He wanted his people to be free to explore these models in private. Over time, this was very useful for his leadership team.

Francois thrived in one-on-one work—he could move with great speed when he could speak, explore, and think without worrying about appearances, spin, advocacy, and so on. There were times when Adam and I would work with Francois in joint sessions. Francois liked hearing us take different points of view; he learned a lot from listening to the ways we would question each other. The disagreements were lively and led to higher-level syntheses.

Francois instinctively knew how to use his thinking partners to bring the game to him and to make it possible for him to play successfully at this new level.

How Do Key Leader Advisory Conversations Evolve over Time?

As you develop from Early Leader to Key Leader, increasingly your choice of thinking partners becomes a defining choice of your leadership. And in fact, it's not one choice, but many: whom you think with, what you choose to think about, what you do with the results of your inquiry. You build the four kinds of thinking partner conversations into the fabric of your leadership. Recall them from Chapter 1: the visionary conversation, the sounding board conversation, the big picture conversation, and the expertise in inquiry conversation.

Let's take a practical look at this.

Expertise in inquiry is where Francois and I began our work, reaching for that third opinion. This is the most common way to begin working with a potential thinking partner—at the working-circle level. As a promising Key Leader, Francois was adept at working with both inside and outside resources at this level. After about four months, the work with Francois evolved into a combination of expertise in inquiry and sounding board. Eventually, after about a year, our work was mostly centered around big picture conversations, and over time Francois developed his ability to come to grips with the strategic business issues in his complex leadership domain.

After about eighteen months of regularly meeting once or twice a month, we both felt it was time for our work to shift again. Mindful that "The road of today can become the ruts of tomorrow," I suggested we take a break to allow Francois to absorb the exponential thinking to date and also to ponder what other thinking partners might best help him with his current challenges.

But I didn't leave the inner circle. Over the next few years, Francois and I would touch base a few times a year, with more frequent contact when he moved to a new position as head of strategy and M&A in another business unit.

Two years ago, Francois was promoted to a new and very complex leadership role in one of the largest business units in his company. He requested that I take a more active role in his inner-circle inquiry, and that we go back to our working model of monthly meetings. It was easy to get back into the groove of our conversations, and this time, we started with big picture and sounding board conversations for six months, while Francois made the transition to his new role and developed his key strategic plans. We then agreed to an ongoing quarterly meeting for the future.

These inner-circle relationships are flexible; there is no one right way. The point is to support the thinking of the leader as needed.

As a Key Leader, you will need to further develop your three Habits, as Figure 20 (page 140) shows. The three Habits will help

	Habit of Mind	Habit of Relationship	Habit of Focus
Early Leaders	Improving exponential thinking Learning to listen	Building base of relationships Experimenting in advisory relationships: give and take	Developing skill in applying insight Balancing personal and professional inquiry
Key Leaders	Developing complete Habit of Mind Balancing internal and external perspectives	Distinguishing inner and working circles of inquiry Building connections between action and inquiry teams	Focusing inquiry on essential nonurgent issues Increasing systematic use of inner circle thinking partners

Fig. 20. Key Leaders focus on building strong inner and working circles of inquiry.

Key Leaders realize the full power of advisory networks and outside insight throughout their careers.

HABIT OF MIND FOR KEY LEADERS

Developing and Using Your Complete Habit of Mind

Having developed the basic capabilities of application, expert, and exponential thinking as an Early Leader, Key Leaders must now turn their full attention to developing their complete Habit of Mind. (See Figure 21.)

By the time you reach the Key Leader level, you will have developed some unique patterns of success. You will have done this by

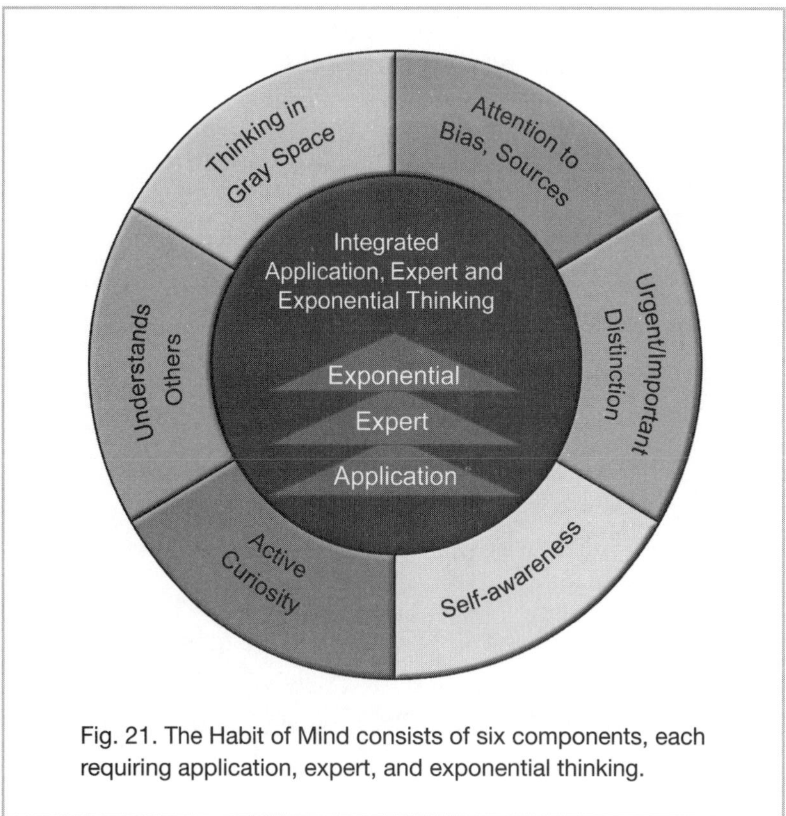

Fig. 21. The Habit of Mind consists of six components, each requiring application, expert, and exponential thinking.

drawing on your curiosity, your self-awareness and awareness of others, different perspectives, and exponential thinking.

The danger is that relying on patterns that lead to success at the Early Leader level often limits or even inhibits success at the Key Leader level. This is one of the well-known causes of executive derailment.[1] For example, this is the point where you make fundamental choices about how much time you'll devote to exploring new ideas. Or how much you will rely on inside information that can be tainted with filters and bias. Or how persistent you will be when making distinctions between urgent and important agendas. Or whether you will continue to work on both your strengths and weaknesses, without becoming smug in your increasing sense of capability, success, ambition, and power.

KEY LEADER QUESTIONS FOR FURTHERING HABIT OF MIND

- How does my active curiosity show up in my day-to-day work? What would my peers say about me? My direct reports? My family?
- How well do I understand and value the abilities of others? How integrated is my understanding of my team and peers with how I frame and approach my own work, as well as direct the work of my reports and division?
- Do I avoid diving into issues where there are likely to be no clear-cut or easy answers? Do I prefer to tackle these issues alone, or do I seek a range of perspectives of others? How systematic is my ability to seek and encourage dissenting views?
- How do I mitigate bias in my information sources? How do I best seek, lead, and integrate exponential thinking on my most important issues?
- What best supports my ability to judge myself from all angles rather than from a single self-interested lens?

The answers to these questions and the choices you make as a Key Leader will ultimately define the kind of leader you can become, now and at the Senior Leadership level.

Balancing Internal and External Perspective

Every company has ways to bring in outside expertise. And every company has a strong set of norms and beliefs concerning how it accepts, reveres, and relies upon outside expertise and capability. Some Key Leaders confuse this with how their company approaches large and visible consulting projects. They miss the ways in which their company may embrace outside insight through barter, exchange, partnerships, or philanthropy. Some companies prefer to bring in extensive outside perspectives as part of education and development programs. Some embed it in recruitment, rewards, or community relationships.

As Key Leaders develop their Habit of Mind, they come to understand that there has to be an appropriate creative tension between internal and external lines of sight. It becomes clear that external resources do not displace internal capabilities, but rather augment and catalyze internal inquiry.

KEY LEADER QUESTIONS FOR BALANCING INTERNAL AND EXTERNAL PERSPECTIVES

- What are my biggest current issues and whom am I thinking with? How varied, how exponential, and how extensive is the nature of inquiry regarding these issues?
- Where do I face the greatest degree of internal bias, filtering, or certainty? Do I need an external perspective to balance those views?

- Where do I face the greatest degree of internal uncertainty and disagreement? What kinds of outside insight would help me resolve those issues?
- Do I have the right type of input for my inquiry and exponential thinking? Are my internal thinking partners pushing me sufficiently? Where are the gaps?
- Do I have external thinking partners who understand the specific issues of my business?
- Which issues in my Star of Complexity Map will be most influenced by external forces? Do I know what I need to know about those issues?

HABIT OF RELATIONSHIP FOR KEY LEADERS

Developing and Distinguishing Inner- and Working-Circle Teams and Levels of Inquiry

Recall from Chapter 4 that it is at the Key Leader stage that the distinctions between inner and working circles become important (Figure 22). This is because now the dimensions of perspective and structural trust are coming more fully into play.

Trust Changes

Most Key Leaders notice early that their move to this level changes relationships. While you may have used your inner-circle action

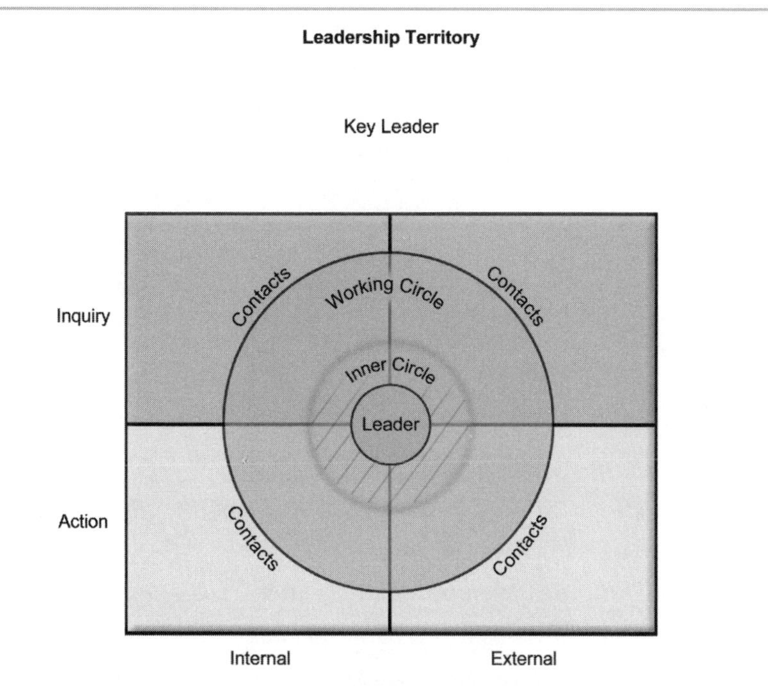

Fig. 22. As you move through the ranks to Key Leader, you will begin to see distinctions between your working circle and inner circle.

team as your primary inner-circle inquiry team in the past, now you will find certain issues hard to discuss with this group. You need to think carefully about why this is. Do you need more honesty from your team, or are there issues of confidentiality, fiduciary responsibilities, or changes in structural trust that have come into play?

While you should work with many people with whom you share medium levels of structural trust, at the Key Leader level you must begin to populate an inner circle (internal and external) focused on your most important areas of exponential inquiry, with whom you share the highest levels of structural trust, as well as high personal and expertise trust. Making mistakes about trust at this level can cost leaders power, influence, and even their positions and reputations.

Key Leaders need to carefully choose members of their inquiry inner circle based on the following criteria:

- Expertise.
- Exponential thinking capacity and complete Habit of Mind.
- Shared personal chemistry.
- Degree of structural trust.
- Relevance to non-urgent important agenda.
- Reputation and relationship to the organization.

As you begin to develop this new inner circle, you should ask yourself, Are my advisers formal or informal, retained or reciprocal, visible or invisible? The right answer is a blend of all of those.

KEY LEADER QUESTIONS FOR CHOOSING YOUR THIRD OPINION TEAM

- Whom can I turn to with my unspoken concerns about an issue or decision?
- Whom would I most want to think with before making my most critical decisions?
- How does my position change the dynamics of structural trust in my leadership circles?
- How do I ensure that my advisers have sufficient perspective to help me test my thinking and commit to a path of action?

- Who can best see problems as broadly as I do? Who challenges my blind spots most effectively?
- Whom do I trust with details that affect both the trajectory of the business and my career? Whom can I talk to with complete candor?

Advisory Network Dynamics

As Key Leaders develop a strong inquiry inner circle, some new dynamics come into play. In addition to reconsidering whom you can trust—and how much—you will need to rethink the close tie between frequency of contact and membership in the inquiry inner circle. This is a new and different dynamic than what's typically true of your action inner circle. First, inner-circle inquiry work looks different than inner-circle action team work. An intense half-day once a month often has enormous impact and leverage. Sometimes meeting once per quarter with intermittent phone and e-mail contact has the same effect. Second, there are stages when it's time to stop working with a particular thinking partner: when issues shift, or when a valuable line of inquiry feels complete. A common characteristic of inner-circle thinking partnerships is that, handled well, these relationships can sustain periods of relative dormancy without losing their inner-circle trust and shared experience. Though they are inactive at times, you can pick up at the same levels of trust as before and get up to speed in very short order.

The accidental component as well as the deliberate component of your advisory network sourcing is also important. You want to leave room for serendipity when developing your leadership circles. Serendipity is important because it can yield relationships with people less like you, people whose perspectives and capabilities are useful to you specifically because of their differences.

Remember, too, as you build your circles, that it is a good idea to broaden your inquiry network. Access to your thinking partners' networks will be a good resource for you in the future.

The Importance of a Network of External Peers

The Key Leader level is also the time to carefully consider the working circle of your external advisory network. Successful leaders typically make a significant investment in developing relationships with a set of external peers. This is critically important for leaders of smaller organizations as well as those in larger ones.

There are a number of ways, formal and informal, to find peers. For many Key Leaders, finding an annual conference or biannual seminar group where participation is limited to a group of industry peers can result in a productive addition to your advisory network. The best of these programs know how to enable higher structural trust than you would likely be able to create on your own. From a peer group like this, you gain a sense of what other people like you are facing. It helps you calibrate your thinking. It helps you develop the ability to understand larger trends in your company, in the marketplace, and in the economy at large. It's a line of sight to early movement, or early warning, about important changes in your industry group.

Leaders of Small to Midsized Companies

Leaders in smaller companies have few, if any, peers to learn from and with. Several organizations have been built specifically to help you do this. YPO (Young Presidents' Organization) and its sister organization, WPO (World Presidents' Organization), are well-known leaders in this field. Joining such an organization gives you access to a large network and the opportunity to become a member in a small inner-circle thinking group. For leaders in small to midsized companies, this is often the best way for you to jump-start the development of your third opinion network and give time and attention to developing your Three Habits. Over time, the dynamics of advisory networks discussed above will come into play. You will likely find that your group is no longer the only inner-circle resource you need for your leadership challenges. Building from this powerful starting point, you must then develop your full inner-circle and advisory network.

Resources for Creating Your Inner Circle

Where will your inner circle come from? We already know that some working-circle thinking partners broaden their roles into inner-circle relationships. At the Key Leader level, you will also need to explicitly cultivate new resources.

Corporate Contacts

At the Key Leader level, it's time to look across and down as well as up. Look for and learn from talent wherever you find it in the business. You can reach out to new employees, whose perspective was shaped by other organizations, and young executives just beginning their careers. You can explicitly cultivate a network of peers to jointly improve common performance and to develop cross-organizational relationships. There may also be Key or Senior Leaders who will be willing to serve as internal inner-circle thinking partners on some issues—for example, a strategist or technologist, corporate counsel, or a person in finance. While often these relationships are bounded by structural trust to the working-circle level, there are many instances where it is possible and desirable for these relationships to evolve.

Alliance/Partner Contacts

As with Early Leaders, Key Leaders operate in an increasingly outsourced and partnered set of business models; thus, leaders at all levels have more opportunity to build bridges across organizations now than at any time in the past. Over time, these relationships can form the basis for a joint and mutually beneficial inquiry. They also are a window onto some of the best people in fields that are related, but not directly competitive with yours.

Family/Partners and Friends

As you distinguish increasingly between working and inner circles, most people turn to the inner circle they already trust: their family and friends. There are both benefits and risks to reaching beyond professional relationships to personal relationships for inner-circle thinking partners. The benefits are obvious: these are individuals with whom you have a long history, whom you trust, and who care about you, are loyal to you, and want to support your success. They are anxious to help you. They are often somewhat external to your specific work environment and can provide one type of external perspective. There are numerous executives whose spouse or family member is a key part of their advisory network. Often, discussing inner-circle business is a way of deepening the inner circle of the personal relationship itself.

The risks are less obvious, but you need to be aware of the potential challenges of turning to your friends and family for third opinions. They can provide invaluable perspective on your management approach and on the translation of your personality into your leadership style—after all, they've seen you in action up close. But they cannot really understand how you are growing and developing expertise and professional capability. In addition, they do not have a disinterested view of you, your organization, or its performance. They defend and protect you, and they see the implications of business issues in personal terms. They also may not have an independent frame of reference for assessing the issues you face, and few opportunities for developing such context.

Turning to a friend or family member as a thinking partner also shifts the nature of the time together. Are you socializing or solving a problem? When does one activity end and another begin? This dynamic can rob leaders of critical relationships that help them take a break from the pressures of work, and sustain and nurture their full lives. The families and friends who have been most successful as thinking partners are those who have established a sense of boundaries. Increasingly, spouses I have interviewed suggest establishing some kind of overarching ground rule that allows them to share inner-circle business conversations but not let them overwhelm personal and family time—for example, limiting conversations about business issues to a weekly session at a favorite coffee shop.

I've spoken to many spouses who say that, while they're happy to take an inner-circle role, what they really wish is that their spouse had more fully qualified people in their trusted inner circle. ("I don't know enough about the business to really be helpful, and I hate how isolated my spouse is when it comes to handling the pressure and making the big calls.") Spouses see the cost of executive isolation in a way that no one else does, and they are acutely aware of the value of expert inner-circle confidants. As much as they want to help, they know that they alone can't fill the difficult void of isolation that seems to come with success.

Contacts beyond the Boundaries

As you work increasingly beyond the boundaries of your organization as a Key Leader, you will uncover potential thinking partners in unusual places: boards of nonprofit organizations, fellow parents at gatherings for your children, social and professional contacts of your spouse.

Peers

As we've discussed in this chapter, cultivating a set of external peers, both inside and outside the organization, is an excellent resource for most key leaders. You may choose, as a Key Leader, to begin to specifically cultivate those relationships to create your inner circle. Shared history can establish a powerful foundation for thinking-partner relationships and can help you calibrate the advice and insight that a thinking partner provides.

Outside Experts and Retained Advisers

Experts typically get to know Key Leaders through the expert work they do, and those relationships may evolve over time into inner-circle thinking partnerships. Being explicit about the evolution of roles is important.

The executives I interviewed were unanimous in voicing their sense that even in working with consultants they know and trust, more than ever they have to be mindful of their consultant's position of vested interest in selling or advocating more services and certain types of solutions. In moving from working circle to inner, and from action to inquiry, structural trust can be a limiting factor in the relationship.

Of course, it is sometimes possible and desirable for an executive and professional services partner to work together to increase structural trust. What you need is a way to take vested interest and advocacy off the table. You can do this (as we saw in the case of Brian Stacey and Jim Corliss) by guaranteeing a certain level of business to the consultant's firm. This potentially frees the partner from his vested interest and enables higher structural trust, particularly if the partner does not lead or get involved in the project work. Another solution is halting any other work the retained adviser's firm may be doing for you.

Smaller consulting firms are sometimes better positioned to provide you with outside insight. Their business model may have flexibility that allows their principals to more easily cross the lines between external action and inquiry, tailoring a combination of both types of work, with the ability to build high structural trust.

You should be aware that, among the independent firms, there are a growing number of companies explicitly designed for third opinion work. These firms understand the kind of structural trust you need for the third opinion and are dedicated to working as advisers and thinking partners without the leverage of project teams.

Another group of thought leaders who are a potential source for external inquiry team members are academics, authors, and conference speakers. It is a time-honored tradition that many highly visible thought leaders serve as advisers and play key roles in the inquiry circles of leaders.

There are a few things to watch out for. First, fame is double-edged—it makes thought leaders visible, but sometimes mitigates structural trust, because once famous, it is harder to work behind the scenes. And the rigors of continuing to build or maintain one's fame are sometimes at odds with the structural requirements of inner-circle thinking partners. Beware also of thought leaders with powerful ideas but little experience in going from ideas to results. For some great thinkers, their gift lies in developing intellectual capital; they are less able to work with people on taking these ideas and tailoring them to their situations.

Broadening Organizational Connections with Your Thinking Partners

A thinking partner works with an individual leader to make the leader more effective within the organization, market, and industry. But the power of an organization lies in its collective wisdom. In the long run, your goal is not to develop isolated individuals at the very cutting edge of inquiry; your goal is to cultivate outside insight that can be translated into results created and realized by teams of people.

Once you're a Key Leader, it becomes increasingly rare that your thinking partners will have no contact with other members of your teams. Of course, there are cases where your thinking partners should remain completely behind the scenes. But in general this is not the case, and you will want to frame and encourage appropriate interaction.

Here's why. First, in order to fully support your thinking, your partners need to have a broad line of sight for your issues. Second, you should develop your people by creating interactions with your best thinking partners. And third, you will enlarge your own reputation by association with top thinking partners.

KEY LEADER QUESTIONS FOR CONNECTING THE THIRD OPINION WITH THE REST OF YOUR ORGANIZATION

- What kind of lines of sight into my realities will build the knowledge and perspective of my thinking partner and increase the effectiveness of our exponential inquiry?
- What kind of interactions with my teams will enable me to move from inner-circle inquiry to effective action?
- What kinds of interactions between my internal and external inquiry teams will energize the inquiry work?
- What kinds of relationships can I encourage among external people who are important to my success?
- What kinds of opportunities are there for my thinking partners to help develop individual thinking of my team members? To support the development of my rising stars?

- What kinds of roles can I ask my thinking partners to take in the larger organization that allow them to discover things I am unable to see or know about? What keeps their interest and knowledge growing?

There are two factors that are critical in building a powerful connection between your thinking partners and the rest of your organization:

- Shaping and empowering the thinking partner's role in relation to the larger organization.
- Your thinking partner's ability to work across the boundary without being drawn into the organizational dynamics.

The challenge in shaping the thinking partner's broader role is this: you want your thinking partner to be close enough to the action to be relevant, while remaining distanced enough to enable effective outside insight. The position of thinking partner, then, is one of standing "next to" as opposed to getting more involved and standing "within."[2]

If your group is facing a challenging new set of ideas, you may want key members of your team to have one-to-one meetings with your adviser (in an expert role). By having the private opportunity to debate, your individual team members can think on their own before working together on difficult problems. This avoids tension or suspicion that can arise in teams that are thrust into thinking together about a hard issue too quickly.

Second, you can ask your thinking partner to join your working group as a content expert, offering an external line of sight that will enhance the group's knowledge.

A third model is to create a *"consigliore"* role, where your thinking partner is available to your high-potential people for their own development and is visible and available within the organization. Of course, to be effective in this type of role, the thinking partner must embody the highest standards of trust and confidentiality, ensuring that no private conversations are inappropriately revealed and that no one is hurt by virtue of his or her presence.

Fourth, if you have an internal group focused mostly on inquiry, such as a strategy or research group, it's valuable to encourage one-to-one expert relationships between your thinking partners and key members of these groups. This can facilitate an easy and valuable cross-pollination of ideas and networks.

The most conspicuous pitfall of engaging your thinking partners throughout the organization, however, is the potential for them to get drawn into corporate politics. For example, a thinking partner should know never to become a go-between. And Key Leaders need to also do their part not to put their thinking partners in this position.

HABIT OF FOCUS FOR KEY LEADERS

Focus Explicitly on Inquiry and Non-urgent Important Issues

The relentless pressure to take action can consume any individual, but it is especially acute as you move into the Key Leader role. People quickly learn that creating urgency is the best way to get and stay on your calendar. Earlier in your career, you might have been lucky enough to have had some free time for idea gathering or reflection. Now, you're going to have to be disciplined and develop your Habit of Focus to make room for this kind of thinking time. If you don't, your schedule will invariably be overrun with day-to-day responsibilities and pressures.

How you spend your unscheduled time is a most significant factor in what kind of results you and your teams will achieve, and what your career trajectory will be.

KEY LEADER QUESTIONS FOR SHARPENING YOUR HABIT OF FOCUS

- Do I have a long-term perspective on my business?
- As I review my Star of Complexity Map, am I focusing my inquiry and exponential thinking on the right issues?
- Do I think through the second- and third-level implications of the big decisions I face? Do I vet this with others?
- Do I specifically consider how to translate big ideas into action in the business?
- Do I insist on a balance of internal and external perspectives in inquiry?
- How broad and diverse are the lines of sight that inform this inquiry?
- Have I looked to see how other leaders in my company and/or people I greatly admire work with others to lift their game? What can I learn from them that I might make use of myself?

You will need a tool to guide the development and on-going iteration of your non-urgent yet important agenda. The Star of Complexity Map (Chapter 5) is one such tool. You may want to have someone serve as the "chairman of your kitchen cabinet" who shares the responsibility for shaping your third opinion agenda and suggesting members of the inquiry team.

Increase Your Systematic Use of Inner-Circle Thinking Partners

Advisory networks in practice are all about balance on three dimensions: internal vs. external, inner vs. working circle, and retained vs. reciprocal. There is no single set of rules that guarantee effective advisory relationships at individual stages of a career. Instead, advisory networks and thinking-partner relationships are shaped by a set of conscious choices about a highly personal and dynamic asset.

KEY LEADER QUESTIONS FOR WORKING WITH YOUR INNER CIRCLE

- Have I developed a personal process (time, structure, thinking partners) for ensuring that I think broadly about the non-urgent, important issues of my leadership, business, and constituencies?
- Do I use the time and energy I devote to inquiry as consistently and effectively as possible?
- What logistics and processes work for me to ensure that I'm getting the value I need from my advisory network relationships?
- Is my network well balanced with relevant expertise and perspectives?

- How and when can I get different groups of my advisers and thinking partners working together?
- How do I position external people in a way that not only works for me, but works for my organization?

It's worth mentioning that working with your inner-circle thinking partners often needs a different kind of time and space than other meetings. A one-hour meeting that starts fifteen minutes late is unlikely to allow for the depth of exponential exploration that is required. Develop the habit of blocking off several hours—often by starting early in the morning or late, with open-ended evening time. And, as tough as this might be, turn off your pager and cell phone!

There are times and circumstances in leadership when a unilateral focus on action is appropriate. Usually these circumstances are driven by urgent need. Staying connected to your inner-circle advisers, even peripherally, during this kind of period is often welcome and uplifting while you deal with the situation. This allows your advisory network to be dormant but not lose momentum, positioning it for fast and easy restart at the right time.

KEY LEADER CHECKLIST FOR YOUR HABIT OF FOCUS

✓ Review your Star of Complexity Map regularly. Rigorously view the star through the three key lenses and, most important, prioritize your needs.

✓ Increase and improve your external relationships, contacts, and resources, so that you can draw on them with confidence.

✓ Develop your inner circle. Begin to work with individual exponential thinking partners.
✓ Continue to ensure that your inquiry shapes successful action.
✓ Manage the inflow of advice, counsel, and information. You don't have to take everything that is offered.
✓ Structure your advisory network to meet your thinking style and needs.
✓ Explicitly allocate time.
✓ Expand the impact of your advisory network to your organization.
✓ Return the favor.

Review your Star of Complexity Map regularly. Rigorously view the star through the three key lenses and, most important, prioritize your needs. You should assess your Star of Complexity Map at some fixed interval—say, quarterly, biannually, or annually. If you find yourself in a period of flux, you may need to return to it weekly. Make sure to get additional perspectives from others.

Increase and improve your external relationships, contacts, and resources, so that you can draw on them with confidence. Explicitly plot your entire network against the critical few elements of your Star of Complexity Map baseline. Use this to identify gaps: Where do you need more external perspectives? Where are you weakest on expert thinking? Where would exponential thinking be most valuable? Given the breadth and interdependencies of the issues that you face now, do you have the right thinking partners to engage with? Where do you need the most rigorous testing of your choices?

Develop your inner circle. Begin to work with individual exponential thinking partners. As you refine your inner circle, start to identify a few key people who might show potential as members of your third opinion team. Do they have the right expertise and chemistry? Do they have the potential to create the right level of structural trust? You can begin to engage in inquiry with current action partners to determine if they'd be appropriate inquiry partners.

Continue to ensure that your inquiry shapes successful action. Balancing when to be in action and when to be in inquiry is an essential juggling act to get right. How much information is enough? How much insight is necessary before you can take action?

Manage the inflow of advice, counsel, and information. You don't have to take everything that is offered. Your single most valuable resource at this level of responsibility is your own time and attention. While an Early Leader should be a sponge, willing to soak in any external perspective or insight, a Key Leader needs to zero in on extracting key information and insight that helps improve performance.

Structure your advisory network to meet your thinking style and needs. Continue to experiment with different types of information flows and different structures for inquiry dialogues and conversations, but make sure that you understand your own needs clearly. You must learn to specify the role that you want your thinking partner to play, in terms of both logistics ("When, where, and how do we exchange information?") and insight ("I want him to challenge my reasoning about this deal. . . . Am I boxing my company in too tightly with the terms I am considering?"), while framing the relationship in a way that allows for unexpected conversations and pursuit of relevant third opinion.

Explicitly allocate time. Don't undermine your exponential thinking and your focus on your non-urgent important agenda by starving it of discussion time. Schedule meetings that are longer than one hour.

Expand the impact of your advisory network to your organization. When the time is right, make the necessary introductions so that your other teams can benefit from the thinking partners you've developed.

Return the favor. As a Key Leader you have already demonstrated success in your career. As a result, you have your own level of expert thinking and have cultivated an exponential thinking capability. You can be an ideal thinking partner for others. First, it will enable you to continue to expand your own inquiry skills by enabling you to ask exponential thinking questions. Second, it will augment your own network through the network of those you advise. Third, it will demonstrate to your organization your commitment to the advisory network as a critical leadership tool.

CHAPTER 9

Senior Leaders

Senior Leaders face a paradox: with greater power comes greater leverage—but the stakes are high and the responsibility higher. Just as the freedom of power becomes greatest, it is perhaps the most circumscribed.

The move to Senior Leader means a whole new level of leadership challenges. You'll now need greater vision, broader focus, and longer time frames. Your actions, and the values embedded in those actions, will be mirrored in your organization. Every move you make will be magnified and scrutinized. Casual comments can become gospel, spread through the grapevine with tremendous speed, and almost certainly distorted along the way. And there is always the possibility that the media will gleefully quote you entirely out of context.

Thanks to this intense scrutiny, Senior Leaders are often heavily protected by well-meaning executives and staff. Unfortunately, this protection can also inadvertently place you in an isolating bubble, separated from the creative and dissident thinking you now need more than ever. The truth will be carefully packaged for you, unless you make it clear that you insist on the unvarnished truth.

In short, you will have a greater need than ever of your advisory network. Gerry Roche, the preeminent executive recruiter of CEOs around the globe, summed it up this way in a recent conversation:

> CEOs want a "kitchen cabinet," a back-door counsel. . . . They are really seeking a sounding board off which they can bounce problems and ideas and get objective feedback. These leaders, strange as it may sound, and as capable as they are, and sometimes being the stars that they are, would prefer to not have to reveal their vulnerabilities or their levels of relative ignorance to their Boards or senior managers. . . . Advisors—to be really effective—tend to operate on a subterranean level of anonymity so that everybody involved is comfortable with the kind of strategic brainstorming and decision analysis that underpins all good leadership decisions.[1]

Recall from Chapter 4 the four signs that you need to reach for the third opinion:

1. "I'm capable of this, but I just don't have time to think about all of it with the right amount of focus."
2. "If I don't get this right, we'll be in serious trouble."
3. "Even if I had the time, I couldn't take on these issues alone."
4. "I can handle this, but how might I accelerate or enable significantly better results if I thought through my options with someone else?"

While you may experience all four signs, at the Senior Leader level, it is signs 3 and 4 that really come into play.

Many Key Leaders can thank their advisory network for helping them get to the Senior Leader level. At this stage, bonds and loyalty on both sides run deep. As the nature of responsibility and power changes at the Senior Leader level, your advisory network needs to grow with the challenges you now face. Figure 23 shows how Senior Leaders use the full power of their three Habits to build their legacy.

To illustrate how advisory relationships change to meet senior challenges, let's examine the relationships among three Senior Leaders and their thinking partners. Each example shows how a Senior Leader draws upon and evolves well-developed Habits of

	Habit of Mind	Habit of Relationship	Habit of Focus
Early Leaders	Improving exponential thinking Learning to listen	Building base of relationships Experimenting in advisory relationships: give and take	Developing skill in applying insight Balancing personal and professional inquiry
Key Leaders	Developing complete Habit of Mind Balancing internal and external perspectives	Distinguishing inner and working circles of inquiry Building connections between action and inquiry teams	Focusing inquiry on essential nonurgent issues Increasing systematic use of inner circle thinking partners
Senior Leaders	Using unusual and diverse thinking to probe broader perspective and complexity Creating a legacy	Having the ability and appetite to explore uncomfortable new ground Using top players and peers in inquiry	Reframing and broadening boundaries of inquiry Making thinking partners powerful in entire organization

Fig. 23. Senior Leaders use the full power of their three Habits to build their legacy.

Mind, Relationship, and Focus to achieve superlative results within the organization.

Leading with the Habit of Mind

In 1998, when Richard Thomas took over the leadership of then troubled Systems Control Corporation, he was already known as an executive who had succeeded in a number of different industries. After earning his MBA from the University of Chicago, he worked in semiconductors, specialty retailing, and computer hardware. He was particularly adept at coming in as an outsider and, within a few weeks, figuring out the core capabilities of a given company.

Richard had done his due diligence by the time he got to Systems. He knew that the company, once premier in its field, had unexpectedly lost money for the first time in its history, and that it was bleeding cash fast. The overall industry was poised for double-digit growth, but not only was Systems not positioned to take advantage of it, the company was positioned to continue to lose. It had squandered an early lead in the days where proprietary lock-in worked; its arrogance showed not only in its customer relationships and service, but even in its pricing strategy. It was clear that mistakes had been made; the question was, what was the right combination of changes that would turn the thing around?

Richard knew he had only a little time to get his arms around the business. He also was well aware that he was a novice in systems control. But Richard viewed his outsider status as an asset as well as a potential liability.

"CEOs become CEOs," he said, "because they have a way of thinking and of framing assumptions about where a company is going that enables successful strategies to be developed and executed.

CEOs remain CEOs when their assumptions are shared by their board of directors and they use them to deliver sustained success."

Richard continued, "External advisers have to know how to think about the future, seeing the dynamics of key variables and markets, and what changes they bring about. People develop lifelong patterns of where they get information and how they arrive at conclusions. Without powerful thinking partners who can provide external input, a vital part of the team is missing."

Richard began to search for an outside systems control expert. He needed someone to provide line of sight into the industry and to get him up to speed on industry issues. He began calling around, asking for advice on finding an adviser. The name Janet Linisfarn kept coming up. Janet, a computer scientist and an expert in systems control software, was well known and respected as an industry expert who served as an adviser to top executives.

Richard arranged a meeting, and within a few hours, he and Janet knew that they could work together. Richard saw in Janet the same ability that he had to sniff out trends. She had a deep understanding of the key drivers in the industry as well as key players—not just companies and individuals but the end users of the software themselves. She knew what made the software work and how the drivers of the industry changed over time. Janet recognized in Richard a dynamic thinker and an executive with more curiosity than she had seen in a long time. She also saw a tough and rigorous mind that invited debate, was willing to be wrong, and loved pursuing discovery and insight.

At first they talked primarily about the market, exploring it, as was Richard's custom, in the context of a three-year time horizon. Policy debates and industry events naturally entered into this dialogue. Janet read everything coming out of Washington, and she became Richard's eyes and ears, albeit with a strong point of view.

Although Janet was originally hired for a three-month stint to bring him up to speed, Richard soon asked Janet to stay and to take on a broader mandate. Their relationship had moved from a working-circle advisory relationship to an inner-circle thinking partnership. Her brief was to provide perspective on any and all market and industry issues she thought they should consider. Richard began to call up to bounce wide-ranging ideas off her. Janet knew everyone in the industry, and her gut reactions were invaluable.

During their early work, she challenged his assumption that he had six months to decide how to bet the company on his strategic turnaround plan. She thought he had six weeks. Together, they sifted data and argued about implications, while thinking in the gray space. In the end, Richard accelerated his time frame to two months.

In the first year, Richard was totally focused on the new direction for the company. With success in hand and the immediate problems fixed, he turned to building a powerhouse. As he worked, he continued to broaden his inquiry with Janet. Richard sent her out as his emissary to visit other firms. She was never an official member of their mergers-and-acquisitions team, but Richard wanted her input as he considered potential acquisitions for Systems.

At other times, Richard asked Janet to work with other members of his team, attending meetings as their resident expert and adviser.

"Executives become committed to seeing from their respective position in their industry," Janet said. "I think of things in a way that executives are 'afraid' to think, because I'm not committed to product, or strategy, or position. That frees me to see the dynamics of their industry as well as other industries, in a way that is different, powerful, and sometimes disruptive."

With Richard and Janet, a relationship that began in expertise in inquiry developed into a vision conversation, with a substantial sounding board component along the way.

Bottom line: in just a few years Richard Thomas took Systems, with a $200 million valuation, and turned it into a company that was acquired at a valuation of $1 billion. With the acquisition, Richard stepped down into retirement.

SENIOR LEADER QUESTIONS FOR DEEPENING HABIT OF MIND

- Now that I've gotten here, how diverse is my inner circle?
- How does my inner circle help me to broaden my perspective and options? Who really makes me think in new ways?
- As I become successful and powerful, am I honest enough to be able to explore uncomfortable truths with my thinking partners?

Broadening Your Habit of Relationship

When I think about Ramon Alicante, I think about someone who has an impeccable Habit of Relationship.

He learned early on, from some very tough assignments in the civil service, that one cannot navigate the tricky waters of leadership alone, so he developed a keen interest in finding and working with people whom he could count on in an ever-expanding network.

Ramon was a student of relationships. He believed that you earn people's trust and loyalty by listening, by being willing to be wrong, by sharing credit, and by making the tough calls swiftly and decisively.

As Ramon rose through the ranks at a major specialty chemicals company, he was transferred overseas. This was a formative experience for him—he learned firsthand how narrow his worldview was. He realized that he had to see himself in relation to a much bigger world than he had imagined before.

And then Ramon got his big leadership break. A division of the company was spun off and he was made the number-two executive. He was ambitious, committed to driving the firm to get superior results. By this time, he had integrated an extensive advisory network into his overall leadership team. One inner-circle thinking partner had helped him develop his abilities to be a global businessperson and had been particularly crucial in working with him on doing business in the Far East. Another inner-circle thinking partner was a financial whiz—Ramon was good enough with numbers, but he learned long ago that he needed an outside and unbiased thinking partner to dig into what was not immediately visible in the numbers with him. Finally, Ramon had a long-standing relationship with someone he thought of as his "big picture pragmatist."

Ramon was confident in his new role but was well aware that he had a lot to learn and that he needed new outside thinking partners. Helping to manage a new publicly traded company brought him face to face with myriad issues he had never experienced during all his years inside the corporate fold.

With his radar set to be on the lookout for potential thinking partners, he met Anesh Rishkamurti at a conference.

From day one Ramon knew he was facing process breaks across silos and regions that caused cost problems and customer dissatisfaction. The manufacturing people and the salespeople were all trying to make their numbers, but they weren't in synch, and everyone was pointing the finger at everyone else. Ramon's first instinct was that it could be fixed by putting better people in charge. But he wasn't sure what really was at the root of the problem.

Ramon needed someone like Anesh to help him get to the bottom of this, someone who didn't have years of history with the players and had no bias as to the root causes. Anesh and Ramon engaged in several conversations that led, not to the answer, but to a highly useful way of framing and testing the issues.

They settled on a multidimensional approach—moving some key people from managing one side of the problem to the other, educating and building alignment for change, getting everyone to see the data in near-real time, and developing a much deeper understanding of customer perceptions. The problems persisted. Because his team was now focused on understanding what was happening without blame or cover-ups, it became clear that the problems were systemic and not fundamentally about the skills or motivation of their people.

Anesh worked closely with Ramon and key members of the team to get to the root of issues. He supported Ramon in getting some of his best people to fundamentally rethink the key assumptions that were now seen as driving the process breaks. Anesh's style of inquiry, and his uncanny knack for finding the piece of a process that was right when it didn't seem to be working optimally overall, helped energize the team and build broad support for the big changes that they implemented fast, with good results.

With this initial challenge under control, Ramon invited Anesh to broaden his focus as a thinking partner, engaging in wide-ranging conversations designed to help Ramon focus on the most important things he could do for the business.

Ramon commissioned a study to analyze what critical performance points would have a positive, nonlinear effect on the company's valuation. Ramon and Anesh spent considerable time thinking about the report, testing, challenging, and asking what-ifs. Over many conversations, they eventually reached a consensus that there was a set of performance points that, while hard to get, would drive a big jump in the company's value. Anesh and Ramon explored all the complex interdependencies inherent in these points, until Ramon was ready to lead his teams through the cycles of action and inquiry that would be necessary to achieve this dramatic increase in operating performance.

"Working with Anesh developed my leadership to full capacity," Ramon said. "Anesh challenged my thinking and made me stretch to see areas I would otherwise not have considered. . . . His expertise, combined with a broad way of thinking, framing, and testing, enabled me to take on the kind of stretch goals that drives big performance. Anesh showed me that there was a whole new level that I was capable of attaining. . . . As I developed more personal confidence in understanding and leading this kind of nonincremental performance shift, I, in turn, could help my organization develop confidence, individually and as a team. It was thrilling to see so many talented people in the company become capable of stepping up to new levels of leadership and performance."

Anesh remained as a mentor and sounding board, helping Ramon think about the new environment in which he was operating, one in which his quarterly results were on display and pored over by analysts.

Anesh's involvement became a turning point in Ramon's Habit of Relationship. While continuing to take on specific issues both as an inner-circle adviser and as a thinking partner, Anesh opened up his own extensive network to Ramon. He enhanced Ramon's networking skills, encouraging him to expand his relationships by serving on other boards.

In an unusual move, Anesh encouraged Ramon to become an informal adviser and thinking partner to the head of a major media company. Initially, Ramon was skeptical, but over time he realized the reciprocal benefit he derived from this broadening of his perspective and how it greatly enhanced his own leadership capacity. Ramon learned what it took to support and push exponential thinking in someone else who is at the top of his game and facing tough choices. In learning more about becoming a good thinking partner to someone else, he understood better what a good thinking partner would look for in him—qualities such as commitment, mutuality, really listening (especially to the things you might not want to hear), and structural trust. He also was able to see how his extensive expertise translated into new situations and reconnected with his intense curiosity and natural questioning when looking at something new and different.

Ramon's experience of the inner-circle thinking partner relationship was so powerful that it gave him a new view of leadership itself. Ramon began to challenge his own people to develop and use their own advisory networks. While he didn't force people to develop outside thinking partners, he came to view effectiveness in this regard as an important criterion as he assessed Key Leaders for promotion.

What ultimately happened to the company? Ramon and his team achieved and exceeded the stretch goals, creating significant value for all their stakeholders. They moved Coatings Worldwide from $150 million in operating profit in year one, to $185 million the second year, to $225 million the third. Along the way, Ramon led the development of a very strong management team, where people individually and as a group raised their skill, their trust levels in each other, and their wisdom about creating extraordinary results—results that mattered.

Ramon and Anesh began working in the big picture, as well as expertise-in-inquiry mode, segued into a sounding board conversation, and ultimately turned their collective attention to matters of vision. Over time, they were fluent in all the types of thinking-partner conversations.

When Ramon stepped down from Coatings Worldwide, everyone expected him to go on to a CEO spot, but he surprised them and himself. He realized that he was more passionate about thinking-partner work. It was hard for his ego to let go of the dream of being CEO, but he felt he was ready to give back, and he knew how much he could offer the next generation of leaders. As a thinking partner, he could choose to work on the issues that he found most interesting, which is not an option when you lead a company. Ramon also felt drawn to the network of advisers and thinking partners he had gotten to know. He found the people interesting, and, through them, he had easy entrée to potential leaders who would benefit from his thought partnership. Today he works with top executives in the Fortune 200 as a thinking partner. He is widely sought for his expertise and networks in the Far East and serves on a number of boards.

SENIOR LEADER QUESTIONS FOR BROADENING HABIT OF RELATIONSHIP

- What do I have to do to get top people to work with me? Is my reputation attractive enough for them to consider me as a thinking partner?
- Do I know how to make thinking partners powerful in the organization?

- Am I sharing ideas with the top players and the unusual thinkers—people I couldn't access before whom I could reach now?
- Whom would I love to meet?

Challenging Your Habit of Focus

Margaret Kaye always meant to leave the industry giant ManuFact, which had hired her twenty years ago—she just never found the time. She was something of a maverick at ManuFact, but—often to her surprise—she found continuing challenges coming her way, interesting assignments, increasing responsibilities, and the sense that ManuFact's role in society was important.

As she became more and more senior, Margaret noticed a pattern of increasing isolation. She could continue to base her day-to-day decisions on quick thinking and intuition, but for long-term business decisions she found herself inundated with information that was no longer black and white but various shades of gray.

When she had been president of a major ManuFact business unit for three years, she was offered the position of group vice president with a much larger portfolio of responsibilities. For the first time, she was brought into the most senior-level conversations about the firm's long-term position and legacy. Deeply disturbed by the insular and political nature of these conversations, she thought they were spending significant time and effort on arranging the deck chairs on a ship that was becoming less seaworthy with each passing voyage. Margaret felt compelled to do something about it.

At this point, she met John Grey. John had served as a thinking partner to the former group vice president. John was well connected and helped Margaret to get grounded in the history and politics behind the deliberations she was now part of. He also helped find peers in her industry to develop new perspectives on some of the issues. But Margaret still felt the need for a different conversation. She believed that ManuFact wasn't asking the right questions about its future and the risks it faced. How would it sustain itself when the factors that made its original rapid growth possible no longer existed? How could the company avoid stagnation or worse? Margaret recognized that ManuFact's internal conversations wouldn't or couldn't address these issues and she needed to breathe some new life into the debate.

Margaret realized she needed to find thinkers well outside the ManuFact mind-set to help her solve her dilemma. She attended a two-day seminar on new methods of dialogue and inquiry, and found the starting point for her new agenda. After the seminar, she continued to bounce ideas around with one of its leaders, Peter, who introduced her to Ben, a leading thinker on long-term sustainability. Peter, Ben, and John began to coalesce as a core team of thinking partners for Margaret. It was Ben who suggested that she needed to hear more. "If you really want to think about sustainability, you must know and listen to a much broader range of perspectives. People from many nations and cultures. People who are artists, teachers, and leaders of nonprofit organizations."

Margaret began what she called a "salon"—a biannual gathering of a diverse group of artists, educators, community leaders, and others whose perspectives were completely outside of ManuFact's normal frame of reference. In addition, she went to worldwide nongovernmental organizations for more formal conversations about the future of ManuFact's industry and its role in world events.

As she worked to profoundly broaden her vision and perspective,

Margaret began to bring along other members of her company to the salons. Her teams were initially skeptical, but quickly became interested and found value in these new activities. Her Key Leaders have started a group salon of their own, and several have developed their own thinking partners.

The bottom line? Margaret developed a cadre of people capable of thinking about long-term positioning and legacy in a new way. Her leadership caused the CEO and board of directors to commission a special committee to develop a blueprint for a sustainable future for the enterprise. Margaret was the senior leadership's top choice to lead this group.

SENIOR LEADER QUESTIONS FOR CHALLENGING HABIT OF FOCUS

- Am I pushing inquiry to the limits regularly? Does this agenda cover the full picture?
- Do the challenges of Senior Leadership cause me to reframe or refocus the boundaries of my inquiry?
- Am I introducing thinking partners appropriately throughout the organization?
- Am I leaving the right legacy?

While Margaret's story is unique, the salons she introduced to her firm are quite common. In the course of my research, I discovered that many Senior Leaders like Margaret have established salonlike events, although they may not have used that name. For instance, a CEO of a diverse conglomerate company holds an annual off-site event that includes people in his "top-fifty" executive team so that they can hear a roster of interesting speakers and thinkers from outside the industry. In choosing his speakers, he particularly looks for diversity of thought, perspective, race, gender, and culture. There are panels and topic sessions and lots of downtime for quiet reflection, chatting, and golf. The participants attend with the understanding that nothing will leak from the meeting, so structural trust is maintained. This CEO notes that three things happen as a result of this annual meeting:

- New ideas flow into the senior team.
- The CEO signals that he brings diversity to the table and expects others to do the same.
- The CEO invites some of the interesting speakers to meet with him during the year, visibly engaging in and signaling support for variety and outside insight.

Another example is the invitation-only CEO summit held annually by Bill Gates and Microsoft. It's a two-day event for top industry CEOs and thought leaders to think out loud together. Bill invites maverick outside thinkers and sets up structural trust in similar ways.

This process—organizing gatherings for inquiry, not just for solving problems—is something that Senior Leaders should support. This creates opportunities to infuse outside thinking into the corporate dialogue, sends a signal that cross-boundary thinking is welcome and desirable, and forms the basis for contacts with people who can develop into advisers and possibly thinking partners over time.

THE SENIOR LEADER WHO LISTENS

What is it about these leaders that attracts and retains their thinking partners? They listen. Moreover, they are willing to step outside their usual comfort zones, and they can handle the unvarnished truth. In the safety of their inner circle, they admit they don't know, aren't sure, and might be wrong. They are more interested in getting it right than in being right. They build lifelong relationships where bonds of loyalty and respect grow deep. They keep things interesting by looking for new ideas.

SENIOR LEADER QUESTIONS FOR EVOLVING YOUR INNER CIRCLE

- Are my inner-circle people the best I can get? How good am I at ensuring that top thinking partners want to work with me?
- Am I really getting the all-important third opinion?
- Are there people I could imagine working with but haven't asked?
- How diverse is my inner circle and how much do they challenge me to think beyond my usual horizons? How comfortable and predictable has my inner circle become?
- What's the right balance of long-term, trustworthy working relationships vs. new blood?
- Do I extend my reach and power into the networks of my advisers?
- Do I ask my thinking partners to take on challenging assignments that force them to think beyond their usual horizons?
- Am I generous in sharing my thinking partners with key people I am developing for future leadership positions? Do I create an environment that encourages others to develop their own advisory networks?

In all of the stories we've seen in this chapter, Senior Leaders faced legacy issues that forced them to think beyond their businesses to the impact of their ideas and actions on their people, the futures of their companies, and the effects on the communities that they and their companies touch.

And so we come full circle: the Habits of Mind, Relationship, and Focus of successful leaders drive the creation of powerful advisory networks, which in turn sustain these successful leaders in their quest to create extraordinary value and realize their full potential and that of their organizations.

A Note on Senior Leaders, Boards of Directors, and Thinking Partners

It's not uncommon in discussions about inner-circle thinking partners to hear the question, "What about boards? Isn't this what the independent directors are for? Aren't they thinking partners for CEOs?" The answer is yes and no. In the best boards, directors are seated because they bring experience, independent thinking, wisdom, and powerful line of sight to the table. CEOs and top management look to their boards for access to their networks as well.

But there are inherent limits to the nature of this kind of thinking-partner relationship. Structurally, board members are not in a disinterested position relative to management. Hiring and firing the CEO is explicitly their responsibility. The board's first and foremost priority is to the shareholders, not the seated management team. What this means, in essence, is that the nature of the director's role precludes the director from becoming too involved with management.

At the same time, directors can and should be working-circle advisers on particular issues. Board members and senior management can and do develop strong relationships. Done well, this is a good thing. At Coatings Worldwide, Ramon developed a close relationship with one of his directors, Bill. Bill was CEO of a company in the transportation-and-distribution industry. In addition to golf and fly-fishing, they shared many deep conversations about the changing nature of the global economics in which their companies operated. The nature of their positions gave them a line of sight to events and market movements that were very useful for pushing each other's thinking. They discussed assumptions and conclusions in research reports they both read and were quick to get in touch with each other if they saw something interesting happening. They greatly enjoyed their intellectual sparring and frank conversation. But Ramon and Bill were very careful. While they engaged in challenging inquiry, they kept this inquiry bounded—looking outward, into global markets and macroeconomic trends. They never discussed business issues of either company, keeping the roles of management and directors appropriately separate.

Interestingly, while structural trust precludes directors from being in the center of the CEO's inner circle, it is not uncommon for directors who initially get to know each other by serving together on a board to develop into thinking partners outside of their roles as board members.

The need for the third opinion extends to board members who carry significant responsibility and risk. They need to have access to information and line of sight that extends beyond what comes in the board packets. At critical junctures in the evolution of a company, directors may need independent expertise and counsel about issues in particular areas, including, for example, governance, technologies, markets, or financial structures. As we saw in the case of Jim Corliss, a CEO's inner-circle thinking partners may also serve in an advisory capacity with directors, though they need to do so with care. Directors may decide to seek advisers who meet with the entire board, or they may choose to access their own networks. Whatever the form, boards interested in the highest standard of governance need to be thoughtful about how they bring outside insight to their work.

Keeping the Relationships Evergreen

Everyone values the deep relationships they have developed over time, but, as comfortable as they are, long-term relationships can lead you into a rut. If you're too comfortable, your inner-circle thinking risks becoming part of a familiar routine, failing to generate the on-going dissonance, questioning, and insight necessary to senior leadership. In order to avoid this, you must explore this reality as an explicit part of the inner-circle conversation.

Are the questions that are uppermost in your mind leading you to think about new possibilities for yourself and your company? Are you maintaining continuity while injecting new thinking? Are you focused on the issues of highest priority and legacy? Do the problems of your leadership mandate remain interesting and challenging for your thinking partner?

A good thinking partner will encourage executives to work with people who have different perspectives. One way to infuse new thinking into the advisory relationship is for the adviser and executive to agree to learn a new area together. A less common but very effective option is for a Senior Leader to frame a challenging discussion, and then ask several advisers to discuss the problem in his presence, but as if the leader were not in the room. This can be very hard for leaders—the temptation to jump in, shape, or rebut some point is hard to resist. After a specified time, the group stops and debriefs with the leader. In my experience, you always learn something unexpected from this kind of conversation.

SPECIAL DILEMMAS OF SENIOR LEADERSHIP

No matter how skilled, dedicated, and intelligent you are, you can't know what you don't know.

You've developed your action teams and you've built your advisory network. You've had the challenging sounding board conversation with your best thinking partners. You've developed a set of possible solutions for a major issue, looked at the solutions from every angle, and yet there is still no obvious rational choice. The facts that would make one or another clearly better or worse are ambiguous, highly interdependent, and not knowable with high certainty, at least not now. So, faced with this gray space, what do you do now?

In his 2001 Harvard commencement address, Robert Rubin, former secretary of the treasury, offered this perspective: "Decisions should not be judged by outcomes but by the quality of the decision making, though outcomes are certainly one useful input in that evaluation. Any individual decision can be badly thought through, and yet be successful, or exceedingly well thought through, but be unsuccessful, because the recognized possibility of failure in fact occurs. But over time, more thoughtful decision making will lead to better overall results, and more thoughtful decision making can be encouraged by evaluating decisions on how well they were made rather than [solely] on outcome."[2]

Faced with the responsibility of making big decisions, your inner-circle thinking partners should help you explore your decision making process so that you can at least be very clear about why you are making the decision you finally settle upon. They will ensure that you leave no managerial stone unturned, that all relevant questions are asked, that data is vetted for bias, and that all the possible interdependencies are considered.

SENIOR LEADERS AND LIFELONG THINKING PARTNERS

In his memoir, Clark Clifford tells of his dilemma in trying to advise President Johnson on Vietnam.[3] Clifford had not been in favor of the troop buildup of the midsixties. However, once the president committed to the policy, Clifford felt that his role as the president's thinking partner was not to continue as a critic, second-guessing the leadership, but, rather, to assist in any way he could to help make the policy work.

There were, of course, other options for members of Johnson's inner circle. Speechwriter and adviser Richard Goodwin, for instance, felt that the Vietnam policy was so seriously flawed that he simply could not participate. He resigned. Later, when Clifford became secretary of defense, he understood clearly that his mandate had fundamentally changed; he was no longer an inner-circle adviser to the president—now he was responsible to the nation rather than to a particular leader. And it was at that point that he resumed his criticism of the war.

Experience and knowledge shared between an executive and a thinking partner is a unique, irreplaceable asset. We all know that the full depth of any relationship develops over time. While rapport is sensed almost immediately, it takes a while to develop trust. Learning how leaders' managerial footprints grow with time and experience, how they typically respond to certain issues, what they're likely to see and not see, what has been successful for them in the past—these are all questions a good thinking partner has to address sooner or later. This knowledge forms the basis for an ever more powerful relationship as the leader faces tough business choices, tough career choices, and tough ethical choices.

The wellspring of exponential thinking and outside insight is new learning, taking on new challenges, and being open to growing individually and as part of a team. The mutual commitment to sustain this wellspring is the hallmark of great thinking partnerships.

CHAPTER 10

Conclusion: Greater than Gold

Only if there is an alternative can you have a choice; make a decision for better or worse, and that will only be possible if an opposite opinion is expressed. It is like gold: you can't tell whether gold is pure unless you strike it against another piece of gold.

—Adviser Artabanus councils Xerxes, king of Persia, as recorded by Herodotus, 5th century B.C.

The life of your inner circle is ultimately about human relationships—how you develop and exercise your fullest capacities when you are pushed and guided by other great people. As David Ogilvy famously said, "If each leader surrounds themselves with people bigger than they are, we will have a company of giants; if each leader surrounds themselves with people smaller than they are, we will have a company of midgets."[1]

The experience and knowledge shared between leaders and their thinking partners form a powerful basis for supporting these leaders as they navigate difficult terrain. Sometimes the ease and comfort of a longtime, highly trusted relationship is what's needed to go into the unknown waters of uncomfortable inquiry, to go beyond what's habitual to new understanding.

Of course, a key objective of inner-circle inquiry is to explore the edges of the habitual, making sure you are not playing yesterday's game in today's world. Much of the exponential thinking that goes on in inner-circle inquiry is all about breaking away from habitual thought patterns, continuing to question, continuing to look for those things, perhaps radically unfamiliar, that might provide greater leverage. When people have experienced all the benefits of such a long-term relationship, they can become *too* comfortable with each other. The quality of thinking and the interaction itself become habitual, which defeats the purpose. Taken to an extreme, an inner circle that once opened new possibilities can create insulation at the top. It's up to you to make sure this doesn't happen.

It's important to remember that insight isn't always immediate. The immediate "Ah hah!" can—and does—happen. Yet some inquiry requires a longer horizon for return on investment.

People who care about—and have a stake in—your leadership don't want you to go it alone. An important factor in how employees at all levels see Senior Leaders is how broadly Senior Leaders think, whom they think with, and how committed they are to learning and change. Early and Key Leaders who participated in my research consistently look for leaders and mentors who integrate the full Habit of Mind with outside relationships that power up their leadership and possibility. People have a great stake in the success of their leaders. They are counting on their leaders' abilities to focus on the non-urgent important issues in the broadest contexts with the best and most challenging thinking.

This is also true of the family and friends of people who shoulder big leadership responsibility; they see executive isolation in a way that no one else does. They understand the personal costs. While they often find a place in the inner leadership circle, they are well aware of their limits in expertise and perspective.

My motivation to begin this research was to improve the decision making capability of business leaders today, but I have found that the habits engendered by this work have effects throughout one's life. Exponential thinking is not limited to leadership issues. Developing your complete Habit of Mind and your ability to understand increasing complexity will change the way you see things in many aspects of modern life. This ability is increasingly called upon in family, social, civic, political, and cultural life.

Developing the full range of your Habit of Relationship will also leave you changed. Understanding and experiencing the power of inner-circle relationships with high structural trust alters your sense of place in the world. The experience of inner-circle inquiry with someone very different from you changes what you expect of yourself and your lifelong development as a person. Inner-circle inquiry is a practice that reinforces your connections and exposes the limits of individual talent. The relationships begun with the thoughtful inclusion of thinking partners in your leadership circle have the power to change the course of your own existence as well as, potentially, many others.

Developing your Habit of Focus changes the way you relate to the myriad demands on your time and energy. Habitually taking the time to reflect about what's really important will reverberate through your entire life, making sure that you make thoughtful and considered choices and don't wake up one day to find you've missed what matters most.

Many leaders who have fully developed the three Habits come to realize that there is something important they wish to do once they step down from their leadership roles. For some, becoming thinking partners to the next generation of leaders is the inevitable capstone of their successful leadership career. But becoming a thinking partner is not for everyone who has attained high levels of leadership. Being able and willing to work behind the scenes is not suited to all leaders.

Having experienced the power of their inner circle, leaders can continue to evolve their inner circle for this new stage of their life, most often focused on legacy, giving back, and lifelong learning.

In the end, inner-circle relationships are unique and precious. They are not disposable or replaceable, even though your inner circle will rightfully change over the course of your leadership and career. They cannot be coerced, and they cannot be bought. These relationships deserve great care and thoughtfulness. The wisdom and joy of living and leading this way is indeed greater than gold.

APPENDIX I: STAR OF COMPLEXITY MAPPING QUESTIONS

WHAT IS MOST COMPLEX AND CHALLENGING ABOUT YOUR ROLE?

- Are there components of this work that are inherently hard and fraught with risk?
- Is a changing global business world creating unexpected and tough challenges?
- Are there fundamental assumptions about the business that must be reexamined?
- Are interdependencies dense and difficult to separate?
- Are there disruptive technologies that need to be understood and harnessed, lest their potential be turned against your franchise?
- Are human dynamics and people issues a major factor?
- What dilemmas are most persistent, perplexing, or pervasive?
- Are your governance systems well aligned with needed action?

- Are there business issues you think about but never have the opportunity to talk about?

WHAT IS MOST COMPLEX AND CHALLENGING ABOUT YOUR FIT WITHIN THE ROLE?

- Do your background and experience serve you in all areas where you need to lead?
- Where are you most uncertain, tentative, or confused?
- How do you keep yourself fresh and invigorated over the long haul?
- What are you most troubled about?
- What are you most passionate about?
- How do you support not only your ability to get results, but also your ability to do your best work?

WHAT IS MOST COMPLEX AND CHALLENGING ABOUT THE WAY YOUR ROLE IS INFLUENCED AND SHAPED BY OTHERS?

- Are there complex human and organizational dynamics at play?
- Are there areas in your star that you know need attention but you hesitate to get into because of the ripple effect this may have on the relative equilibrium between you and your peers or boss?
- How capable is your organization to react to change with speed and flexibility?
- How do metrics and decision patterns affect organizational behavior?[1]

APPENDIX II: THIRD OPINION QUESTIONS FOR EARLY, KEY, AND SENIOR LEADERS

Think about your current leadership circles and ask yourself:

- What kind of contacts and network have I built, and how and when do I use them?
- Are there teachers, mentors, friends, and activities that have been particularly important in my development at some stage in my life?
- How do I include my spouse or significant other, family members, and personal friends in my current leadership circles?
- When have I had a conversation or ongoing dialogue where I significantly changed my understanding or learned something I did not expect? What were the conditions and nature of the relationship that led to the insight?
- Are there critical areas for me now where I have no thinking partner, or where the thinking partners I have are lacking in expertise, perspective, or appropriate structural trust?

EARLY LEADER QUESTIONS FOR IMPROVING EXPONENTIAL THINKING

- Are there things that I see as clear-cut issues that someone four levels above might see from many perspectives and not as being so clear-cut? Do any of these issues directly affect my excelling at work today?
- Are there issues or challenges that seem persistent or recurrent despite my best efforts to work on them? What are the underlying dynamics that seem to keep me from making progress on these issues?
- Are there things that I know that top management doesn't know that, if they did, would lead them to make very different decisions? What prevents them from knowing these things? What's useful and not useful about their not knowing?
- Are there people I'm working with whose behaviors just don't make sense to me? Is there something about how they see the world that might be very different from my own background and understanding?
- How much flexibility do I have to structure my time? Do I use my time as effectively as possible? How long is the time horizon I'm working on?
- Have there been things that have happened that were totally unexpected? What do I now do differently to not be caught unaware?
- Are there people who think about things and frame questions in ways that are better than I can, and whom I admire? What makes them able to do that?

EARLY LEADER QUESTIONS FOR BUILDING YOUR BASE OF RELATIONSHIPS

- In addition to the day-to-day interactions, are there people you are more interested in knowing over time?
- Are there things you would do differently if you thought these people would be in your leadership circle for the long haul?
- What happens when some of these people are no longer in your day-to-day world?
- How effective are you at cultivating and maintaining relevant contact with people when you are not in active contact on daily issues?

EARLY LEADER QUESTIONS FOR GETTING RESULTS FROM INSIGHT

- Is there a pattern in how you go about trying to use new insight?
- How well do you understand the full range of stakeholders for your new idea?
- How often do you see a new idea through to a result? How often do such ideas slide onto the list you never get to?
- How do you calibrate which ideas are most likely to have a big impact?
- How easy is it for you to get sidetracked?

EARLY LEADER HABIT OF FOCUS CHECKLIST

- Use the Star of Complexity Map to frame and focus your advisory relationships.
- Identify potential resources and reach out to them.
- Experiment with the characteristics of advisory relationships that would be most useful to you.
- Establish a time commitment.
- Work on using the insights.
- Set milestones for considering the state of your advisory network and revising or reminding yourself of next steps.
- Renew the cycle.

KEY LEADER QUESTIONS FOR FURTHERING HABIT OF MIND

- How does my active curiosity show up in my day-to-day work? What would my peers say? My direct reports? My family?
- How well do I understand and value the abilities of others? How integrated is my understanding of my team and peers with how I frame and approach my own work, as well as direct the work of my reports and division?
- Do I avoid diving into issues where there are likely to be no clear-cut or easy answers? Do I prefer to tackle these issues alone, or do I seek a range of perspectives of others? How systematic is my ability to seek and encourage dissenting views?

- How do I mitigate bias in my information sources? How do I best seek, lead, and integrate exponential thinking on my most important issues?
- What best supports my ability to judge myself from all angles rather than from a single self-interested lens?

KEY LEADER QUESTIONS FOR BALANCING INTERNAL AND EXTERNAL PERSPECTIVES

- What are my biggest current issues and whom am I thinking with? How varied, how exponential, and how extensive is the nature of inquiry regarding these issues?
- Where do I face the greatest degree of internal bias, filtering, or certainty? Do I need an external perspective to balance those views?
- Where do I face the greatest degree of internal uncertainty and disagreement? What kinds of outside insight would help me resolve those issues?
- Do I have the right type of input for my inquiry and exponential thinking? Are my internal thinking partners pushing me sufficiently? Where are the gaps?
- Do I have external thinking partners who understand the specific issues of my business?
- Which issues in my Star of Complexity Map will be most influenced by external forces? Do I know what I need to know about those issues?

KEY LEADER QUESTIONS FOR CHOOSING YOUR THIRD OPINION TEAM

- Whom can I turn to with my unspoken concerns about an issue or decision?
- Whom would I most want to think with before making my most critical decisions?
- How does my position change the dynamics of structural trust in my leadership circles?
- How do I ensure that my advisers have sufficient perspective to help me test my thinking and commit to a path of action?
- Who can best see problems as broadly as I do? Who challenges my blind spots most effectively?
- Whom do I trust with details that affect both the trajectory of the business and my career? Whom can I talk to with complete candor?

KEY LEADER QUESTIONS FOR CONNECTING THE THIRD OPINION WITH THE REST OF YOUR ORGANIZATION

- What kind of lines of sight into my realities will build the knowledge and perspective of my thinking partner and increase the effectiveness of our exponential inquiry?
- What kinds of interactions with my teams will enable me to move from inner-circle inquiry to effective action?
- What kinds of interactions between my internal and external inquiry teams will energize the inquiry work?

- What kinds of relationships can I encourage among external people who are important to my success?
- What kinds of opportunities are there for my thinking partners to help develop individual thinking of my team members? To support the development of my rising stars?
- What kinds of roles can I ask my thinking partners to take in the larger organization that allow them to discover things I am unable to see or know about? What keeps their interest and knowledge growing?

KEY LEADER QUESTIONS FOR SHARPENING YOUR HABIT OF FOCUS

- Do I have a long-term perspective on my business?
- As I review my Star of Complexity Map, am I focusing my inquiry and exponential thinking on the right issues?
- Do I think through the second- and third-level implications of the big decisions I face? Do I vet this with others?
- Do I specifically consider how to translate big ideas into action in the business?
- Do I insist on a balance of internal and external perspectives in inquiry?
- How broad and diverse are the lines of sight that inform this inquiry?
- Have I looked to see how other leaders in my company and/or people I greatly admire work with others to lift their game? What can I learn from them that I might make use of myself?

KEY LEADER QUESTIONS FOR WORKING WITH YOUR INNER CIRCLE

- Have I developed a personal process (time, structure, thinking partners) for ensuring that I think broadly about the non-urgent, important issues of my leadership, business, and constituencies?
- Do I use the time and energy I devote to inquiry as consistently and effectively as possible?
- What logistics and processes work for me to ensure that I'm getting the value I need from my advisory network relationships?
- Is my network well balanced with relevant expertise and perspectives?
- How and when can I get different groups of my advisers and thinking partners working together?
- How do I position external people in a way that not only works for me, but works for my organization?

KEY LEADER CHECKLIST FOR YOUR HABIT OF FOCUS

- Review your Star of Complexity Map regularly. Rigorously view the star through the three key lenses and, most important, prioritize your needs.
- Increase and improve your external relationships, contacts, and resources, so that you can draw on them with confidence.
- Develop your inner circle. Begin to work with individual exponential thinking partners.

- Continue to ensure that your inquiry shapes successful action.
- Manage the inflow of advice, counsel, and information. You don't have to take everything that is offered.
- Structure your advisory network to meet your thinking style and needs.
- Explicitly allocate time.
- Expand the impact of your advisory network to your organization.
- Return the favor.

SENIOR LEADER QUESTIONS FOR DEEPENING HABIT OF MIND

- Now that I've gotten here, how diverse is my inner circle?
- How does my inner circle help me to broaden my perspective and options? Who really makes me think in new ways?
- As I become successful and powerful, am I honest enough to be able to explore uncomfortable truths with my thinking partners?

SENIOR LEADER QUESTIONS FOR BROADENING HABIT OF RELATIONSHIP

- What do I have to do to get top people to work with me? Is my reputation attractive enough for them to consider me as a thinking partner?
- Do I know how to make thinking partners powerful in the organization?

- Am I sharing ideas with the top players and the unusual thinkers—people I couldn't access before whom I could reach now?
- Whom would I love to meet?

SENIOR LEADER QUESTIONS FOR CHALLENGING HABIT OF FOCUS

- Am I pushing inquiry to the limits regularly? Does this agenda cover the full picture?
- Do the challenges of Senior Leadership cause me to reframe or refocus the boundaries of my inquiry?
- Am I introducing thinking partners appropriately throughout the organization?
- Am I leaving the right legacy?

SENIOR LEADER QUESTIONS FOR EVOLVING YOUR INNER CIRCLE

- Are my inner-circle people the best I can get? How good am I at ensuring that top thinking partners want to work with me?
- Am I really getting the all-important third opinion?
- Are there people I could imagine working with but haven't asked?
- How diverse is my inner circle and how much do they challenge me to think beyond my usual horizons? How comfortable and predictable has my inner circle become?

- What's the right balance of long-term, trustworthy working relationships vs. new blood?
- Do I extend my reach and power into the networks of my advisers?
- Do I ask my thinking partners to take on challenging assignments that force them to think beyond their usual horizons?
- Am I generous in sharing my thinking partners with key people I am developing for future leadership positions? Do I create an environment that encourages others to develop their own advisory networks?

NOTES

1. The Essence of Outside Insight

1. R. Kegan, *In Over Our Heads: The Mental Demands of Modern Life* (Cambridge: Harvard University Press, 1994).
2. C. Clifford, *Counsel to the President* (New York: Random House, 1991), pp. 423–24.

3. Habit of Mind

1. C. Argyris and D. Schön, *Organizational Learning: A Theory of Action Perspective* (Reading, Mass.: Addison-Wesley, 1978); and P. Senge, *The Fifth Discipline* (New York: Doubleday, 1990).
2. D. Goleman, *Emotional Intelligence* (New York: Bantam Books, 1995).
3. H. Gardner, *The Mind's New Science: A History of the Cognitive Revolution* (New York: Basic Books, 1984).
4. C. Fitzgerald and J. Berger, *Executive Coaching: Practices & Perspectives* (Palo Alto, Calif.: Davis-Black Publishing, 2002).
5. P. Pande, R. Neuman, and R. Cavanagh, *The Six Sigma Way: How GE, Motorola, and Other Top Companies Are Honing Their Performance* (New York: McGraw-Hill, 2000).
6. C. Argyris, *Overcoming Organizational Defenses: Facilitating Organizational Learning* (New York: Prentice Hall, 1990).

7. C. Hampden-Turner, *Building Cross-Cultural Competence: How to Create Wealth from Conflicting Values* (New Haven: Yale University Press, 2000).
8. C. Christensen, *The Innovator's Dilemma: When New Technologies Cause Great Firms to Fail* (Management of Innovation and Change Series) (Boston: Harvard Business School Press, 1997).
9. P. Schwartz, *The Art of the Long View: Paths to Strategic Insight for Yourself and Your Company* (New York: Doubleday, 1991).
10. R. Martin, *The Responsibility Virus: How Control Freaks, Shrinking Violets—and the Rest of Us—Can Harness the Power of True Partnership* (New York: Basic Books, 2002).
11. D. Ciampa and M. Watkins, *Right from the Start: Taking Charge in a New Leadership Role* (Boston: Harvard Business School Press, 1999).
12. D. Markova, *The Art of the Possible: A Compassionate Approach to Understanding the Way People Think, Learn and Communicate* (York Beach, Maine: Conari Press, 1991).
13. J. Katzenbach and D. Smith, *The Wisdom of Teams: Creating the High-Performance Organization* (Boston: Harvard Business School Press, 1993).
14. Clifford, *Counsel to the President,* p. 424.

4. Habit of Relationship

1. M. Gladwell, *The Tipping Point: How Little Things Can Make a Big Difference* (Boston: Little, Brown, 2000), p. 54.
2. R. Heifetz and M. Linsky, *Leadership on the Line: Staying Alive through the Dangers of Leading* (Boston: Harvard Business School Press, 2002).
3. J. Welch, *Jack: Straight from the Gut* (New York: Warner Books, 2001).

5. Habit of Focus

1. S. Covey, *Seven Habits of Highly Effective People* (New York: Simon & Schuster, 1989).
2. With thanks for the insights and conversations with Joe Fuller, Monitor Group.

8. Key Leaders

1. M. Lombardo, *Preventing Derailment: What to Do before It's Too Late* (Greensboro, N.C.: Center for Creative Leadership, 1989).
2. With thanks for the insights and conversations with Juanita Brown, Whole Systems Associates.

9. Senior Leaders

1. With thanks for the insights and conversation with Gerald Roche of Heidrick and Struggles.
2. R. Rubin, Harvard University commencement address, 2001.
3. Clifford, *Counsel to the President*.

10. Conclusion: Greater than Gold

1. D. Ogilvy, *The Unpublished David Ogilvy* (New York: Crown Publishers, 1986).

Appendix 1. Star of Complexity Mapping Questions

1. With thanks for the insights and conversations with Judy Brown, University of Maryland.

INDEX